To Russ,

Happy travels!

[signature]

7 - 20 - 2019

FLUSHED WITH CURIOSITY

101 travel tales with a twist

Western

Eastern

Don Knebel

Thanks to Lori Robertson for her dedication and help.

All photographs by the author, except the back cover photograph of the author, taken by Jen Knebel

Published & distributed by:
Donald E. Knebel

in association with:
IBJ Book Publishing
41 E. Washington St., Suite 200
Indianapolis, IN 46204
www.ibjbp.com

Library of Congress Control Number: 2015948790
ISBN 978-1-939550-29-3
First Edition
Printed in the United States of America

Dedication

To Jen, whose inspiration, sense of adventure and unconditional love and support are the real stories behind this book.

Foreword –
Starting from the Bottom

Eastern-Style Toilet in India

In 2009, my wife and I spent almost three weeks in India. We visited the Taj Mahal, palaces, the place where Gandhi started his peaceful revolution and dozens of other sites we will never forget. But we also went into rural villages to interact with regular Indians. When nature's call came, we often found little more than a hole in the floor, with a water hose sometimes hung nearby. If we didn't want to use the hose for its intended purpose, we had to carry our own tissue. We got used to the idea of throwing our tissue into a little basket placed near the hole for just such a purpose.

I assumed that once people in such remote places learned about the western miracles of flush toilets with seats and squeezably soft paper, they would quickly abandon their old ways. So I was surprised when we were about to leave the airport in New Delhi. Identical doors near the security lines marked "Eastern" and "Western" were not the names of airlines. Many of the passengers, whose familiarity with western culture was reflected in their stylish jeans and sneakers, chose the door that opened to a hose and a hole in the floor. Not recognizing how condescending this sounded, I asked our guide why so many Indians still preferred the "Eastern" door. His answer was as matter of fact as it was enlightening – "It is hard to convince many people here that it is appropriate to sit on a seat that someone else has just used. Besides, that is why God gave us left hands." I had no more questions.

In trips both before and since our visit to India, we have seen places that many Americans will never see. Keeping in mind what I learned about Indian toilets, I have tried to find stories in the places we visit that exhibit not only our common humanity but the traditions and religious beliefs that both unite and divide us. This book is the result of that effort. But nothing more about toilets.

Contents

The Walls of Jericho

Stone Tower in Jericho, Palestinian Territories

Jericho, in the Palestinian Territories, is best known as the city where Joshua "fit the battle" and the "walls come tumblin' down." Archaeologists cannot confirm that famous Biblical story, but did unearth a tower from the very beginning of civilization that held a world's record for more than 5000 years.

Located in the Judean Desert, Jericho is known as the "City of Palms" because of its lush landscape, watered by underground springs. Nomads attracted by the springs founded Jericho in about 10,000 B.C., creating one of the world's first permanent settlements. By about 9400 B.C. the residents of Jericho erected the world's first city walls, protecting themselves from hungry thieves. Archaeologists have uncovered more than 20 successive Jericho settlements, each built over the ruins of the one before, eventually creating a six-acre mound (tell) of dirt and rubble.

In the 1930s, John Garstang, an archaeologist excavating at Jericho, uncovered walls that had suddenly collapsed, which he believed demonstrated the truth of the Biblical account. In the 1950s, Dame Kathleen Kenyon, a British archaeologist, made a systematic study of Jericho's walls and concluded that they had fallen, perhaps as the result of an earthquake, hundreds of years before the presumed date of Joshua's battle. She also concluded that Jericho was not occupied at the time of Joshua. Subsequent investigations have confirmed her conclusions, which few scholars now challenge.

During her excavations, Dame Kenyon found a cylindrical stone tower about 26 feet high and 28 feet in diameter just inside the oldest Jericho walls. The tower, incorporating an internal stairway, has been dated to at least 8000 B.C., making it perhaps the world's oldest man-made structure. Archaeologists originally thought the tower had defensive or irrigation functions, but recent studies suggest it marked the summer solstice. Whatever its purpose, the Jericho tower remained the tallest man-made structure in the world until about 2650 B.C., when it was surpassed by the stepped pyramid of Djoser in Egypt.

The walls of Jericho probably didn't "come tumblin' down" as the old spiritual celebrates. Jericho is nonetheless important to understanding how human beings first began creating what we now call civilization.

Secret of the Pyramids

Step Pyramid of Djoser at Saqqara, Egypt

Egypt's larger than life pyramids continue to generate speculation about their origins, ranging from the extraterrestrial to the supernatural. Even the Egyptians once posited a divine explanation. The so-called "step pyramid" at Saqqara shows that the real story is closer to Earth.

Believing that souls live on after death, Egyptians initially buried their important dead and their possessions in underground tombs covered by *mastabas. Mastabas,* made first of mud bricks and then of stones, were solid, flat-topped structures up to 30 feet high, having gradually sloping sides. A passage to a special chamber inside allowed priests and family members to bring offerings to the person buried below for use in the afterlife.

In about 2650 B.C., Imhotep, the palace architect of Pharaoh Djoser, came up with a new idea for his boss's tomb at Saqqara, the burial ground serving the Egyptian capital at Memphis that is now part of a UNESCO World Heritage site. He covered the underground tomb with six stacked *mastabas* of increasingly smaller size, creating a stepped pyramid made entirely of stone.

After seeing the step pyramid, in about 2600 B.C., Pharaoh Snefru wanted his pyramid to eliminate the steps and support his body above the ground, to be closer to the sun god. About two thirds of the way to the apex, engineers had to reduce the angle of inclination from 55 degrees to 43 degrees to eliminate stability problems created by the internal tomb chamber. The result was the so-called "bent pyramid." On the next try, Snefru's engineers started with a 43-degree angle and succeeded in creating the first "true pyramid," with smooth sides and a constant angle. This "red pyramid" may contain still secret passages leading to the undiscovered mummy of Snefru. Using Snefru's model, his son Khufu took the pyramid building art to its pinnacle in the Great Pyramid of Giza, still the most massive structure ever built.

No little green men, no magical powers, no unsolvable mysteries. Egypt's pyramid builders drew on past successes, learned from earlier mistakes and achieved lasting greatness. That is the secret of the pyramids.

A Flying Boat?

Solar Boat in Boat Museum in Cairo, Egypt

The Boat Museum on Cairo's Giza Plateau was built to display a single item—a 4500-year-old wooden boat. The boat's purpose is not known, but it may have been designed to fly.

In 1954, archaeologists discovered 1224 neatly arranged pieces of cedar wood in a pit carved in the bedrock just south of the Great Pyramid of Khufu (also called Cheops), the pharaoh who ruled Egypt from about 2589 to 2566 B.C. After studying ancient shipbuilding techniques, workers eventually reassembled the pieces into a boat 142 feet long and 20 feet wide. The cedar planks are held together with vegetable rope, which was also buried in the pit. With no place for a sail, the flat-bottomed boat came equipped with six pairs of oars, the pair at the rear used for steering.

The shape of the boat, with an elongated prow and stern suggesting lotus stalks, resembles so-called "solar boats" shown on ancient Egyptian drawings transporting the sun god on his daily journey across the sky. Since Egyptians believed deceased pharaohs accompanied the sun god on his travels, some Egyptologists have speculated that the boat was buried, like the pharaoh's other earthly possessions, for the pharaoh to use in the afterlife. But a disassembled boat seems an odd choice for a deified pharaoh to use while traversing the heavens and the boat shows evidence of having been in earthly water before being disassembled and placed in its pit. So the boat may have been used to transport the body of Khufu down the Nile from his capital in Memphis to his tomb in the Great Pyramid before it was disassembled and buried to prevent its reuse by mere mortals. Or perhaps the boat was used by Khufu for trips along the Nile to greet his subjects.

Whatever its original purpose, the world's oldest intact boat is as seaworthy as the day it was built, a tribute to the skill of ancient boat builders. Khufu's reassembled boat is now displayed near his Great Pyramid in a building part of the UNESCO World Heritage site.

Steeple Chase

Temple in Luxor, Egypt

Among the many delights of a trip to Egypt are visits to its many well-preserved temples, including the one in Luxor typically seen at night. But no matter how well preserved the temples, they are all missing at least one of the matched pair of obelisks, some more than 100 feet tall, which once flanked their entrances. The missing obelisks were not lost—they are in Europe, some standing in front of famous churches. And while the obelisks are missing from Egypt, their spiritual descendants stand in front of places of worship around the world.

For ancient Egyptians, the obelisks' gently sloping sides and gold-plated crowning pyramids probably symbolized the paths of sun rays streaming toward Earth, representing the connections between the sun god and the temple. To reflect the eternal nature of those connections, Egyptians carved their obelisks from a single piece of granite, weighing hundreds of tons. Visitors to the quarry at Aswan can still see the famous "unfinished obelisk," abandoned thousands of years ago when a crack was discovered in the granite, making it useless for its intended purpose.

When Romans conquered Egypt in the first century B.C., they were so enamored of the obelisks that they pulled them down from the temples and sent them to Rome on specially designed ships. Today, there are more Egyptian obelisks in Rome than in Egypt. One is in front of St. Peter's Basilica, a cross now extending from its apex. The largest one, also with a cross on top, is in front of St. John Lateran's Basilica, the seat of the Pope. The obelisk now in the Place de la Concorde, the largest public square in Paris, came from the Luxor temple, which some people have said now looks like an elephant missing a tusk.

Many churches, mosques and Hindu temples have tall, slender structures near their entrances, often topped with pyramids, pointing toward the heavens. Some, like the magnificent riverside Coptic Christian cathedral in Aswan, the birthplace of obelisks, feature a matched pair. These steeples, minarets and towers continue to reflect the Egyptian idea of an eternal connection with the divine.

Crete Expectations

The Original Labyrinth near Heraklion, Crete

The inhabitants of Crete, the largest Greek island, have long suffered a strange libel. But they got the last laugh when scholars learned that Crete was the heart of an advanced civilization existing hundreds of years before civilization came to the Greek mainland.

The Biblical letter to Titus says that "Cretans are always liars, evil brutes, lazy gluttons." Michelangelo's famous Sistine Chapel scene of the Last Judgment shows the legendary Cretan King Minos, with a serpent wrapped around him, judging the damned as they fall into hell. This painting was based on Dante's *Inferno*, in which Minos is depicted with a snake for a tail directing souls of the dead to their proper locations.

In 1900, English archaeologist Sir Arthur Evans uncovered on Crete the ruins of the ancient Minoan civilization at Knossos, previously known only in legend. Modern travelers to Knossos, near modern Heraklion, can visit the restored palace complex. That large complex, built between 1700 and 1400 B.C., contained more than 1300 interlocking rooms on multiple levels. It is the likely source of the ancient story of the labyrinth, where King Minos is said to have kept the half-bull, half man Minotaur.

The Minoans were the original sea-farers, with ships carrying both goods and culture around the Mediterranean. Life-size plaster reliefs found at Knossos reflect the imported Egyptian ideal of people shown in profile. Exported Minoan pottery has been found as far east as the Mediterranean coast of modern Israel. In fact, some people think that the Philistines who settled along that coast were actually Minoans who fled Crete when a volcanic eruption destroyed their cities, perhaps giving rise to the legend of Atlantis.

Cretans and King Minos have regained their good reputations. But the Greek Islands were not created equal. If you long to see where European civilization really began, where the Minotaur was kept, and where the legend of Atlantis may have started, a trip to Crete would be a great choice. But if you imagine a Greek island with gleaming white villages on a hilltop above bright blue waters, you should probably stick with Santorini.

A Liberated Woman

Pharaoh Hatshepsut's Mortuary Temple at Deir el-Bahri, Egypt

Near the entrance to Egypt's Valley of Kings is a magnificent 3500-year-old temple that even today is considered a model for adapting a building to its surroundings. But Hatshepsut, the powerful female pharaoh honored by this mortuary temple, was unknown until the twentieth century. Her successors had tried to erase not only her memory but her very existence.

Hatshepsut was born in 1508 B.C., the daughter of Pharaoh Thutmose I. After a brief stint as regent for a young male pharaoh, Hatshepsut declared herself pharaoh in 1479 B.C. During her reign, she dressed as a man, even wearing a false beard strapped around her head. One of the most successful rulers of her era, she greatly expanded Egyptian trade and engaged in a massive building program unmatched for centuries. One of the many buildings she constructed was her mortuary temple at a complex now called Deir el-Bahri, dedicated at her death in 1458 B.C.

Like other pharaohs, Hatshepsut made sure that the walls of her colonnaded mortuary temple contained numerous images of herself and hieroglyphic representations of her name. Egyptians believed that their *ka*, the essence of their being, could live on after their deaths in a physical representation of the deceased, such as an image or an inscribed name.

Pharaohs ruling after Hatshepsut tried to eliminate any place for her *ka* to reside. They destroyed her statutes, obliterated her images on temple walls and erased her name from everything they could find, including lists of pharaohs. Scholars believe these pharaohs saw depriving Hatshepsut's *ka* of a place to live as a way to restore *Ma'at*, the natural order of the universe they thought had been upset by their female predecessor.

Twentieth century archaeologists reconstructed Hatshepsut's lost reign from images overlooked for destruction. Her mummy, found without markings, was identified in 2007 when a tooth known to be hers matched the mummy's empty socket. Hatshepsut's mummy now lies alongside those of other great pharaohs, all men, in the Cairo's Egyptian Museum. Many would say the true natural order has finally been restored.

Fame from Obscurity

Valley of the Kings near Luxor, Egypt

In about 1500 B.C., 1000 years after construction of the famous pyramids of Giza, the Egyptians began burying their pharaohs in the so-called "Valley of the Kings," now a UNESCO World Heritage site. The best known of the dozens of pharaohs entombed there was actually one of the least important, which ironically explains his current fame.

The Valley of the Kings is on the west bank of the Nile River near the modern city of Luxor, called Thebes by ancient Egyptians. The site was apparently selected because of the large pyramid-shaped rock overlooking the valley. The area's relatively soft limestone allowed workers to dig steep shafts extending hundreds of feet to underground burial chambers enclosing a giant stone sarcophagus. Along all the walls and ceilings, artisans painted elaborate scenes of the pharaoh's life and life with the gods and instructions on how to answer questions at the final judgment. The pharaoh's earthly possessions were buried with him for later use if, as expected, his *ka* survived that judgment.

To prevent looting the entrances to the tombs were scattered around the valley and concealed behind tons of limestone. But the camouflage did not work and the tombs were systematically raided as security lessened with Egypt's declining resources in about 1100 B.C. Tomb raiders checked off the pharaohs as they found each tomb and eventually concluded they had found them all.

But they missed a pharaoh named Tutankhamen who had died at age 19 after a short reign and had apparently been omitted from the dead pharaohs lists. The discovery of King Tut's tomb in 1922 created a worldwide sensation. Today, 3500 items of gold and other rich materials found in his tomb are the primary attraction of the Egyptian Museum in Cairo. Unlike all the other pharaohs, King Tut's mummified body is still in his never-raided tomb.

The Valley of the Kings is open to the public and entry to the now well-lighted tombs is permitted on a rotating basis to protect their magnificent art from crowd damage. The small tomb of King Tut, undisturbed for 3300 years, is a tribute to the benefits of obscurity.

Rewriting the Bible

Ugarit Temple of Ba'al, near Litakia, Syria

In 1928, a Syrian farmer stumbled into a tomb near the modern Mediterranean coastal city of Litakia. The tomb was part of the ancient Canaanite city of Ugarit, one of the most important cities in the western world from about 1500 to 1200 B.C. The excavation of Ugarit led not only to a revision of history but to a literal rewriting of the Bible.

Archaeologists digging at Ugarit found a tablet about the size of a finger containing thirty unique characters, one for each day of the lunar month, originally formed in wet clay with a wedge-ended stick. Although the writing instrument was the same as that used in other forms of cuneiform writing, the characters were not. Instead, each character represented a unique vocal sound and could be strung together with other characters to create words. Until this discovery, the invention of the alphabet had been attributed to the Phoenicians, who lived further down the coast and about 500 years later. Today the tablet from Ugarit containing the first alphabet is on display in the National Museum in Damascus.

The Ugarit excavators also found the ruins of a temple, once visible from the Mediterranean. About 5000 clay tablets, written in a language similar to Hebrew, told stories of the Canaanite god of war and weather named Ba'al who was worshipped in this temple. The Ugarit tablets cleared up a great Bible mystery. The English translators of the King James Bible did not know the meaning of "Asherah" and decided to translate it as a "grove," leading to incomprehensible statements about burning "vessels that were made for Ba'al, and for the grove." Relying on the discoveries at Ugarit, modern translations simply use the name "Asherah," noting that she was a Canaanite goddess.

The temple of Ba'al can still be seen in Ugarit, along with boat anchors left by sailors grateful for steady winds and calm seas. Statues of Ba'al and his father El, found among the Ugarit ruins, are now in Syrian museums. The fertility goddess Asherah again has her rightful place in the Bible.

Triads and Trinities

Pharaoh Ramses II with Horus, Isis and Osiris at Abydos, Egypt

The Great Temple at Abydos is famous for its richly detailed scenes of Egyptian gods. Some of those scenes include images that some people have associated with the Christian doctrine of the Trinity.

Abydos, the burial site of pharaohs as early as 3000 B.C., later became connected with Osiris, a legendary pharaoh considered god of the afterlife. Popular stories told how Osiris had been killed and then miraculously fathered the falcon-faced god Horus with his sister/wife Isis. Pharaohs saw themselves as earthly manifestations of Horus and aspired to live on like Osiris after their deaths.

In about 1280 B.C., Pharaoh Seti I built a temple on the west bank of the Nile at Abydos to honor himself and the triad of Osiris, Isis and Horus. Reliefs show Seti I with Osiris, depicted with a curved beard reflecting his death; Isis, crowned with the sun disk; and Horus, shown holding a cross-shaped *ankh*. Seti's son, Ramses II, expanded the temple, showing himself with the Abydos triad in similar, but less well-executed, scenes. The well-preserved temple walls also contain a unique list of earlier pharaohs, minus the female Hatshepsut and the short-lived Tutankhamen.

When the Greeks conquered Egypt, they took home from Abydos images and stories of Osiris, Isis and Horus. Isis became popular throughout the Greek and later Roman world as the "Queen of Heaven" and "Mother of God." The Roman Catholic Church later adopted these titles for Mary, the mother of Jesus. Christian artists sometimes depicted Mary as Isis, with an Egyptian-style sun crown. Early paintings of Mary with Jesus on her lap mimicked temple scenes of Isis nurturing young Horus. As a result of these titles and images, some people have mistakenly concluded that the Christian Trinity consists of the Father, Son and Mary.

The carvings in the temple of Seti I, the finest remaining examples of Egyptian bas relief, are reason enough to visit Abydos. Seeing the bases for reconstructing the order of pharaohs and for confusion over the Holy Trinity is a bonus.

They Moved the Mountains

Temples at Abu Simbel, Egypt

Ramses II, called Ramses the Great by history, is the pharaoh most often associated with the exodus of the Israelites from Egypt under the leadership of Moses. Although Ramses lived for 90 years and ruled Egypt for 66, he could not get enough of himself. And so, throughout his reign he built one after another self-serving monument, many surviving for more than 3000 years thanks not only to the extraordinary technology of his age but to that of our own.

The most impressive monument Ramses built to himself is at Abu Simbel, then at the southern edge of his kingdom and now a short plane ride from Aswan. Skilled workers literally hollowed out a small mountain to create a multi-room temple both honoring Ramses and warning outsiders not even to consider invading a kingdom with such a powerful ruler. To make sure everyone got the message, four 65-foot-tall seated statues of Ramses were cut from the mountain at the temple's entrance. Just inside, in a hall honoring Ramses' military exploits, eight columns also cut from the rock showed Ramses as the god Osiris. Rooms further into the mountain had more statues showing Ramses as a god. A temple to Nephertari, the favorite of his many wives, was carved into a nearby mountain, showing her as the goddess Hathor along with other statues of Ramses.

Today, the water of Lake Nasser, formed in the Nile River by the Aswan High Dam, nearly covers the mountains at Abu Simbel in which Ramses carved his temples. Archaeologists initially proposed giving underwater tours. Fortunately, some clever engineers had a better idea. Beginning in 1964, workers, supported by UNESCO, cut the temples, statues and surrounding rock into more than 10,000 blocks, some weighing 30 tons. They moved the numbered blocks to a site 200 feet higher and 600 feet further from the Nile and re-assembled them using a metal dome for support, even faithfully recreating a fallen Ramses statue at the entrance. The boundaries between the blocks are largely invisible and visitors not knowing the history often don't notice anything out of place. Ramses II, the most prodigious builder in Egyptian history, would be proud.

Where is Mt. Sinai?

St. Catherine's Monastery in Sinai Peninsula, Egypt

Visitors to Egypt's Sinai Peninsula can explore one of the world's oldest monasteries, housing what is claimed to be the burning bush in which Yahweh first appeared to Moses. They can then ride a camel up nearby Mt. Sinai to see where Yahweh gave Moses the Ten Commandments. But both the bush and the mountain may be in the wrong country.

Exactly where God met Moses has never been clear. One passage in the Hebrew Scriptures locates the site on Mt. Horeb. Such uncertainty over Biblical places was unsettling to Roman Emperor Constantine, who accepted Christianity in about 312 A.D. So he sent his mother, Helena, to the Middle East to determine where events in the Bible occurred.

Helena returned claiming to have found the cave in Bethlehem where Jesus was born, the spot in Jerusalem where he was crucified and the still-living bush in Egypt where Moses met God. Constantine ordered a chapel built around Helena's bush and sixth century Emperor Justinian I surrounded the chapel and its famous bush with St. Catherine's Monastery, now a UNESCO World Heritage site.

Over the years, at least three mountains near St. Catherine's have been designated Mt. Sinai. The current bearer of the name was selected in the sixteenth century based on a tradition of the local Bedouins, who now run the camel rides. Muslims, who also believe that God delivered his laws to Moses on Mt. Sinai, call this mountain *Jebel Mūsa*, the mountain of Moses.

Skeptical scholars say Helena made a big mistake. They note the Bible locates Mt. Sinai in an area called Midian, which, unlike the Sinai Peninsula, was never part of Egypt. They believe that Mt. Sinai, if it exists, is probably a volcano in Saudi Arabia.

For visitors to Sinai, whether the mountain called Mt. Sinai has anything to do with Moses may not be that important. Following the narrow path toward the summit on the back of a camel is a unique and exhilarating experience in its own right. And St. Catherine's, in addition to its bush, holds some of the oldest existing manuscripts of the Christian *New Testament*.

Ark of the Covenant?

Holy of Holies in Edfu Temple of Horus in Egypt

People have long speculated about the fate of the Ark of the Covenant the Bible says the Israelites carried during their Exodus from Egypt. Although of no help on that question, a well-preserved Egyptian temple may provide clues about the origins of that famous box.

The Temple of Edfu was built by the Greek rulers of Egypt beginning in the third century B.C. to honor Horus, the falcon god of the sky. Following the model of much earlier temples, a small statue of Horus resided in a niche in the temple's Holy of Holies, accessible only by the pharaoh and the high priest. Priests occasionally transported the god statue away from the temple in an ark (box) resting in a miniature boat carried on two poles. A replica of the ark now displayed in the Holy of Holies is based on a wall relief showing the ark with its poles sitting on a pedestal in a boat floating on the Nile. On the relief, two bird-like creatures face each other above the ark, their wings extending over the seat on which Horus sat.

So what does Edfu's Ark of Horus have to do with the Ark of the Covenant? According to the Bible, the Ark of the Covenant, enthroning Yahweh, the invisible Jewish God, was carried on two poles attached by rings to the base. The Ark incorporated two cherubim facing each other, their wings extending over the mercy seat from which Yahweh spoke. When the Israelites built their Temple in Jerusalem, they ensconced the Ark in its Holy of Holies, which the Jewish High Priest entered once each year. Jewish soldiers carried Yahweh in the Ark as they went to battle the Philistines.

The Temple of Edfu was built long after the Exodus. So the Ark of Horus might have drawn on descriptions of the Ark of the Covenant. The striking resemblances could be coincidental. However, temples erected before the Exodus contain similar, less-well-preserved, images of arks transporting Egyptian gods. It seems likely that the Israelites, as they left Egypt, carried their invisible God in an ark similar to the ones with which they were familiar.

Philistines in Egypt

Wall at Medinet Habu, Egypt, Showing Ramses III Battling the Sea People

The well-preserved mortuary temple of Ramses III at Medinet Habu celebrated the pharaoh's earthly achievements and allowed priests to nourish his soul so he could live forever as a god. The temple is best known for wall carvings providing information about the Philistines, nemeses of the ancient Israelites after they entered their Promised Land.

Ramses III ruled Egypt from 1186 B.C. until his death in 1155 B.C. Colorful columns in the hypostyle hall of his 150-meter-long temple near Luxor show Ramses among the gods. Statues in a courtyard portray him as Osiris, god of the afterlife. Wall carvings show him delivering enemies to Amun, Egypt's highest god at the time.

The most famous carvings are on the north exterior wall. They portray Ramses, bow stretched, and his troops battling a confederation of invading sea people, predominantly people the Egyptians called "Pelesets" and the Bible calls Philistines. The carvings show the Philistines riding three-man chariots pulled by two horses, wielding double edged swords and long spears, carrying round shields and wearing feathered headdresses. According to the hieroglyphic account, Ramses defeated the invaders, taking many of them prisoner. The carvings also show women and children in ox carts, suggesting an entire population on the move.

Most scholars believe the sea people described at Medinet Habu left the Aegean Sea area in about 1200 B.C. for reasons unknown and sought to settle in Egypt. After Ramses III beat them back, they moved into nearby areas. The Philistines took what is now the Gaza Strip area along the eastern Mediterranean coast. According to the Bible, as the Israelites entered their Promised Land they stayed clear of the Philistines, apparently because of their superior iron weapons and fighting skill. The Philistines later moved aggressively into Israel's heartland until young David killed their champion Goliath and they retreated to five cities along the coast.

The Philistines are remembered today in the name "Palestine," first used by Herodotus in the fifth century B.C. to describe the area that is now Israel. They are also remembered on the wall at Medinet Habu for battles that help shed light on much more recent events.

Valley of the
Shadow of Death

St. George's Monastery in Wadi Qelt, Palestinian Territories

Wadi Qelt (or Kelt) is a narrow gorge cutting through the Judean Wilderness, a rugged mountainous area in the West Bank east of Jerusalem. A blue-domed monastery improbably clinging to its steep northern face marks Wadi Qelt as a special place, not only the setting for one of Jesus' best known parables but also the likely inspiration for the Bible's best loved Psalm.

For thousands of years, travelers between Jerusalem and Jericho have followed the 17-mile long path through Wadi Qelt, facing danger from falling, wild animals, and thieves hiding in its many caves. By the time of Jesus, the Romans had built a road through Wadi Qelt that became the setting for the only parable of Jesus tied to a specific geographic location. The traveler rescued by the Good Samaritan had been beaten by thieves and left to die by passing countrymen along this dangerous road to Jericho.

Shepherds can still be seen above Wadi Qelt, leading their sheep and goats along paths worn into the hillside by countless earlier shepherds. The shepherds still guide their flocks along these paths with their rods and still lead them to the calm, spring-fed waters of the Wilderness. When sitting above Wadi Qelt, it is impossible not to imagine that the writer of Psalm 23 was sitting in the same spot when he wrote about his Lord, the shepherd, protecting and comforting his animals as they walked through the "valley of the shadow of death." Whether this really happened will never be known, but it is easy to see the comforting words of that famous Psalm as an effort by their writer, traditionally thought to have been David, to connect his image of God with the real experiences of his people.

A trip to Israel and the Palestinian Territories includes many opportunities for connecting the events in the Bible with the locations where they happened. But few travel experiences compare with sitting above Wadi Qelt and contemplating the hundreds of generations that have experienced both its dangers and the words of hope and compassion it may have inspired.

Honoring God's Wife?

Holy of Holies of Temple at Arad, Israel

Arad was an ancient Canaanite city lying in the south of modern Israel, between the Negev and the Judean wilderness. Well-preserved ruins of the city, now a national park, go back to about 2600 B.C. The Arad ruins are most famous for their suggestion that Jewish residents of ancient Israel worshipped both God and his wife.

According to the Bible, Moses initially tried to lead the Israelites into their promised land in Canaan from the south, through the area around Arad. The Canaanite King of Arad aggressively resisted their entry, capturing some prisoners. Because of this interference with what they saw as God's mandate for their occupation of the land, the Israelites promised God that if he allowed them to enter Canaan they would destroy the Canaanites and their cities. When the Israelites eventually entered Canaan from the east, crossing the Jordan River just north of the Dead Sea, they proceeded to do precisely that, starting in Jericho.

In about 1200 B.C., the Israelites built a fortress at Arad near the original Canaanite city. In 1962, archeologists unearthed a temple within the fortress, dating to the time of King Solomon and built to honor Yahweh, the invisible God of the Israelites. Because the temple in Jerusalem has not been found, this is the only Jewish temple from the Biblical period ever uncovered. Like the Jerusalem temple described in the Bible, the Arad temple had a large altar of undressed stones in the courtyard. Like the temple in Jerusalem, the Arad temple had a Holy of Holies surrounding a four-horned altar for honoring Yahweh once each year by burning incense. But unlike the temple in Jerusalem, the Arad temple encompassed a second incense burner, smaller than the first. Arad's Holy of Holies also included two standing stones, apparently representing two deities.

Scholars believe Arad's second incense burner and second standing stone probably honored Asherah, the wife of the supreme Canaanite god El whose name is reflected in many Jewish names, including Israel. The Israelites could destroy the Canaanite cities. They could not so easily destroy the Canaanite belief that even God needs a wife.

The Last Battleground?

Jezreel Valley from Megiddo, Israel

The excavated ruins of the ancient city of Megiddo, a UNESCO World Heritage site, overlook Israel's Jezreel Valley. Based on a single and ambiguous statement in the Bible, millions of people believe Megiddo and the Jezreel Valley will be the site of a climactic battle between good and evil.

The Jezreel Valley, a triangular-shaped inland valley south of the Sea of Galilee, has been part of an important trade route between Egypt and the empires of southwest Asia for thousands of years. The Romans, who also used the route for military campaigns, called it the "way of the sea." Competing empires trying to control intercontinental trade have fought at least 34 battles in the Jezreel Valley, the first one in the fifteenth century B.C. when Pharaoh Thutmose III fought the King of Kadesh. In the twentieth century A.D., the Allies fought the Ottoman Empire there.

Since about 7000 B.C., the city of Megiddo has controlled access to the Jezreel Valley. The Bible reports that King Solomon fortified Megiddo, along with the cities of Gezer and Hazor. Excavations at Megiddo have uncovered a tenth century B.C. chambered gate very similar to those found at Hazor and Gezer, lending support to that account. Archaeologists, digging through 26 layers of ruins, have also found evidence of administrative buildings and storehouses from the time of Solomon and a concealed tunnel built in the ninth century B.C. that gave Megiddo residents access to their water supply during sieges. Megiddo was permanently abandoned after 586 B.C. when the Babylonians captured Jerusalem.

The *Book of Revelation* reports that unnamed kings will be gathered together at Armageddon just before the return of Jesus, presumably to prepare for battle. The word "Armageddon" is a translation of the Hebrew "*har megiddo*," or "mountain of Megiddo," an apparent reference to the large earthen mound or tell that eventually formed over the abandoned Megiddo ruins. Relying on this passage, Christians since the first century have predicted one final battle in the Jezreel Valley, almost always involving the most hated regimes of their eras, from the Romans to Saddam Hussein's Iraq. The wait goes on.

Making History

Wall of Karnak Temple Near Luxor, Egypt

A famous temple complex near Luxor, Egypt, now a UNESCO World Heritage site, includes decorated walls thanking the gods for enabling their military successes. One of those walls dates the reigns of Biblical Kings David and Solomon.

In about 2000 B.C., Pharaoh Sesostris ordered construction of a new temple. For 1300 years, his successors kept building on the site until the complex of temples, halls and obelisks now called Karnak had grown into the largest collection of religious structures in the world. Amun was one of the most important of the gods worshipped at Karnak. An annotated wall drawing shows Amun delivering about 150 captured cities, each identified by hieroglyphs, to a pharaoh named Sheshonk (or Shoshenq). The cities include Arad, Beth-She'an, Megiddo and other cities of ancient Israel. Scholars recognized that the Karnak wall memorializes an Egyptian campaign against "the fortified cities of Judah" the Bible says succeeded because King Rehoboam had abandoned the laws of Yahweh, the God of Moses. The Bible identifies the conquering pharaoh as Shishak, which scholars say is another name for Sheshonk. So we have two records of the same military campaign, with only the god mandating the outcome differing between them.

Using Greek and Egyptian records, scholars have determined that Sheshonk ruled Egypt from about 943 to 922 B.C. Somewhat arbitrarily, they have dated his campaign against Judah to 925 B.C., three years before his reign ended. Since the Bible says the campaign occurred in Rehoboam's fifth year, his father Solomon must have passed the throne to him in 930 or 931 B.C. Because Solomon reigned for 40 years, his father David died in about 970 B.C.

Jerusalem is missing from Karnak's long list of captured cities. The Biblical version of Sheshonk's campaign (2 *Chronicles* 12) provides the reason. Sheshonk (or Shishak) spared Jerusalem (and Rehoboam) in exchange for "the treasures of the temple of the Lord [Yahweh] and the treasures of the royal palace."

For people curious about whether events described in the Bible really happened, a visit to Karnak can provide some insight. It also provides an opportunity to view some truly spectacular ancient structures.

Proof of King David

Canaanite City Gate at Tel Dan, Israel

Underground springs and runoff from Lebanon's Mount Hermon create a lush landscape in the Galilee Panhandle of northeast Israel far different from the arid remainder of the country. This fertile area includes Tel Dan, a large archeological mound named for the Biblical Tribe of Dan that produced one of the most important archaeological finds in Israel's history.

In about 1800 B.C., the Canaanites established a major city called Laish in the region around Tel Dan. Archaeologists have uncovered a mud brick city gate from that period that includes the oldest known arched opening, an invention once incorrectly attributed to the much later Romans. According to the *Book of Joshua*, members of the Tribe of Dan conquered Laish after their exodus from Egypt because the Philistines prevented them from capturing the land near the Mediterranean coast originally assigned to them. Archaeologists have unearthed stone gates and walls from the period of Israelite occupation of Dan, which the Bible says formed the northern boundary of the United Monarchy ruled by King David. Visitors can also explore the excavated "high place" the Bible says Jeroboam built in Dan when the northern Kingdom of Israel split from the southern Kingdom of Judah after the death of David's son, Solomon. Dan's high place, featuring a golden calf, competed for worshippers with the Temple in Jerusalem.

During excavations at Tel Dan in 1994, archaeologist Avraham Biran discovered pieces of a broken stele (monument) erected by King Hazael of Aram-Damascus in the late ninth century B.C., boasting of capturing Dan and killing Israel's King Jehoram. Most scholars now believe the Aramaic writing on the stele also says Hazael killed Ahaziah, "son of the king of the House of David," the first non-Biblical evidence of David's existence.

Although the now famous Tel Dan stele confirms the historicity of David and his dynasty, it contradicts the Biblical account of the Israelites' battle with Hazael. According to the *2 Kings*, Jehoram and Ahaziah were killed in a coup after the battle by their general Jehu, who then became king. Even details in battle reports can reflect their author's point of view.

Will London
Lose its Marbles?

Section of Parthenon Frieze in London's British Museum

Magnificent marble sculptures from the Parthenon are among the most popular of the eight million items in London's British Museum. These so-called "Elgin Marbles" are also the museum's most controversial items, with persistent claims they were plundered from Greece.

Pericles built the Parthenon atop the Athens Acropolis in the fifth century B.C. to house a colossal statue of the goddess Athena. The colonnaded building, visible throughout the city, was the epitome of classic Greek architecture, adorned inside and out with exquisitely carved marble figures and friezes. As Athens later fell to different empires, the Parthenon was converted to a church and then a mosque and finally an ammunition dump. In 1687, gunpowder stored by the Ottomans exploded during a battle with the Venetians, severely damaging the Parthenon. The artwork was strewn amid the rubble.

In 1798, Thomas Bruce, the seventh Earl of Elgin, became British ambassador to the Sultan of the Ottoman Empire, then controlling Athens. Initially desiring only to make casts of the art he found in the Parthenon ruins, he later decided to take it home. Whether he wanted the pieces for his Scottish estate or to prevent further damage is still disputed. Whatever his motive, he obtained a controversial document from the Sultan purportedly giving him permission to remove "stones" from the Acropolis. Interpreting the document to permit the removal of anything made of stone, Lord Elgin personally spent 70,000 pounds to remove and ship to England about half of all the artwork of the Parthenon, including 17 pediment statues, 15 exterior panels called metopes depicting mythical battles, and 250 feet of the frieze honoring the Olympian gods that originally extended around the interior. Apparently needing money, he sold the items to the British government in 1816 for 35,000 pounds. Since the 1850s, the word "Elginism" has been used to describe cultural vandalism.

The Elgin Marbles are now displayed in British Museum's Duveen Gallery, a large room built especially for them. The Greek government has repeatedly demanded their return as stolen art, a claim the British government has rejected. UNESCO has offered to mediate the dispute.

Tales of the Crypts

Treasury of the Pharaoh at Petra, Jordan

One of the most anticipated "surprises" in all of travel is at the end of the *siq*, the long and narrow split in the sandstone that suddenly opens to Petra's Treasury of the Pharaoh, hewn from the cliff face and glowing pink in the sun. Pockmarks in the stone urn above the classic portico reflect the unsuccessful efforts of local Bedouins to get at the gold they believe the Pharaoh stored there after chasing the Israelites all the way from Egypt. There was never any money in the Treasury and the Pharaoh of the Exodus missed Petra by almost a thousand years.

Petra, the Rose-Red City in southern Jordan, was founded in about 400 B.C. by the Nebateans at the center of the caravan routes then crisscrossing the Middle East. The Treasury was actually the tomb for an important Nebatean king. A second impressive carved façade called the Monastery, reached by climbing more than 800 steps through steep mountains, was another tomb. Petra has so many elaborately carved tombs that some people have speculated that it was really a city of the dead, reserved for burials and religious ceremonies. However, a 6000-seat theater carved among the tombs and shops along a cardo (main street) lined with columns prove otherwise. At its peak, Petra was probably home to 30,000 or so people, nurtured by an ingenious system that captured and directed water from flash floods.

Petra was annexed to the Roman Empire in 106 A.D. and later contained a Byzantine church with spectacular mosaics. The Crusaders in the twelfth century used the Monastery as a church, leading to its current name. Having been lost to the West for centuries, Petra was "rediscovered" in 1812 by a Swiss explorer masquerading as a Bedouin.

Petra, a UNESCO World Heritage site, was recently named one of the new Seven Wonders of the World and is definitely worth the trip. But don't expect to find the impressive rooms and statues behind the Treasury's façade shown in *Indiana Jones and the Last Crusade*. Like the gold in the urn, they exist only in the imagination.

Bagpipes and *Keffiyehs*

Bagpipers at Southern Theater at Jerash, Jordon

The Roman ruins at Jerash, 30 miles north of Amman, are among the best preserved of any ancient city. Because of meticulous restorations, visitors can almost imagine they have returned to the second century, making Jerash the second most popular tourist destination in Jordan.

People have lived near Jerash for more than 6500 years, but the city remained small until it was conquered by the Roman Empire in 63 B.C. and joined the Decapolis, the league of cities mentioned in the Bible. Known as Gerasa, the city prospered from trade with Petra and began building temples, baths and theaters. When Emperor Hadrian visited in 129 A.D., Gerasa erected a three-opening arch in his honor and began a golden age of prosperity. Eventually, the city encompassed 200 acres, with a population of about 20,000. When Christianity became legal in the fourth century, Gerasa residents defaced the temples and built churches.

After Persia conquered Gerasa in 614, the city began a slow decline. In 749, Gerasa was virtually destroyed by an earthquake and the ruins were eventually buried under blowing sands and forgotten. When the ruins were rediscovered in 1806, the building materials had not been looted as in other ancient cities, allowing reconstruction of structures from the recovered rubble. Today, after almost 100 years of continuous effort, Hadrian's arch, temples to Zeus and Artemis, two theaters, public baths and fountains, markets and a hippodrome have been at least partially restored. The half-mile-long cardo ends at an unusual 90-meter-long paved oval surrounded by Ionic columns, whose original purpose is still uncertain.

Each July or August, entertainers from around the world celebrate their cultural connections with ancient Rome in the restored southern theater during the Jerash Festival of Culture and Arts. Every day, robed Jordanians in red *keffiyehs* serenade visitors to the southern theater with bagpipes. Surprising to many, bagpipes are authentically Roman. Early writings describe Nero playing the *tibia utricularis*, its pipes probably sewn to the leg and head openings of a sheep skin. The Scots borrowed the idea from invading Roman soldiers. Where the *keffiyehs* came from is another story.

Cleopatra's Temple

Cleopatra and Caesarion on Temple of Hathor in Dendera, Egypt

Visitors to the Dendera temple of Hathor experience one of the best preserved of all Egyptian temples. They also see a rare image of one of the most fascinating women in history.

When Alexander the Great died in 323 B.C., his general, Ptolemy, founded a pharaonic dynasty that ruled Egypt for almost 300 years. Like Alexander, the Macedonian Greek pharaohs of the Ptolemaic Dynasty believed they were gods and built temples celebrating themselves and their achievements. In about 55 B.C., Ptolemy XII began erecting a temple to Hathor, the Egyptian goddess of fertility and beauty, on the site of earlier temples near the town of Dendera, 37 miles north of Luxor. Heroic reliefs carved on temple walls were apparently intended to represent Ptolemy XII, but he died before the images were identified with him.

Ptolemy XII was succeeded in 51 B.C. by his daughter, Cleopatra VII, who charmed her subjects by learning the Egyptian language. Cleopatra displayed other charms when Julius Caesar visited Egypt in 48 B.C. She had herself delivered to him in a rug, leading nine months later to a son nicknamed Caesarion (Little Caesar). Cleopatra was forced initially to share power with her brother, Ptolemy XIII, who was eventually killed trying to escape forces loyal to Cleopatra and Caesar. Cleopatra added her deified image to the rear wall of the Dendera temple, depicting herself as Hathor accompanying Caesarion, her chosen successor, pictured as pharaoh.

After Julius Caesar was assassinated in 44 B.C., Cleopatra seduced Mark Anthony and bore three of his children. According to first century Jewish historian Josephus, Cleopatra also attempted to seduce Biblical King Herod, who rejected her advances when he visited Egypt in 40 B.C. After Cleopatra's suicide in 30 B.C., Romans under Octavian (Augustus Caesar) killed Caesarion, ending the Ptolemaic Dynasty. Roman emperors, including Trajan, then enhanced the Dendera temple. Emperor Nero, who saw himself as a god, added his likeness to the temple walls.

The Dendera temple of Hathor, surprisingly intact after more than 2000 years, is a superb example of Greco-Egyptian temple architecture. Seldom-seen images of Cleopatra and Caesarion are an additional treat.

Hidden Meaning

Cave 4 at Qumran, near the Dead Sea in Israel

In 1946, Bedouins exploring caves near Jericho found the first of the Dead Sea Scrolls. Who wrote them and why they were hidden is still disputed, but their effect on understanding first century Jewish beliefs is undeniable.

Archaeologists searched near where the Bedouins found the first seven scrolls and eventually discovered more than 950 complete manuscripts and fragments in 11 additional caves, with so-called "Cave 4" yielding the largest cache. Some scrolls include at least portions of all the books of the Hebrew Scriptures except *Esther*, pushing the dates of the oldest known copies of those books back about 1000 years. Others contain recognized books not in the Hebrew Scriptures, including *Jubilees* and 1 *Enoch*. The most interesting scrolls include previously unknown Jewish writings, some describing a mysterious Teacher of Righteousness. Scroll 4Q521, evoking *Isaiah* 61, says a coming Jewish Messiah "will heal the wounded, and revive the dead and bring good news to the poor." That prediction is the earliest known writing explicitly linking the expected Messiah with the resurrection of the dead, a concept important to early Christians.

After finding the Dead Sea Scrolls, archaeologists excavated the nearby ruins of Qumran, unearthing a narrow room, ceremonial baths, pottery and inkwells. Some scholars are convinced Qumran was home to the Essenes, a strict first century Jewish sect, who wrote or copied the scrolls in their scriptorium. Qumran guides recite this idea, speculating that John the Baptist may have been an Essene. Others argue, with equal conviction, that Qumran was a villa, a fortress or perhaps a pottery factory having no connection with the scrolls, which they claim were hidden by people fleeing Jerusalem before its fall in 70 A.D. Others believe the scrolls were written at Qumran, but not by Essenes.

No matter who wrote the Dead Sea Scrolls, their discovery has added greatly to understanding the diversity of Jewish thinking about the Messiah at the time of Jesus. Their discovery has also spurred a new interest in the Essenes, known from the writings of first century historian Josephus but largely ignored because of the Biblical emphasis on the Sadducees and Pharisees.

Awaiting the Messiah

Cemetery on Jerusalem's Mount of Olives

Jerusalem's Mount of Olives has been important to Christians since the first century. Jesus met with his disciples among its olive trees, prayed with them near its base at Gethsemane and ascended to heaven from its peak near Bethany, sites all now marked by churches. For even longer, the Mount of Olives has been important to many Jews, who still seek to be buried along its slope.

The Mount of Olives lies across the Kidron Valley from the eastern wall of the Temple Mount. According to Jewish tradition, the Messiah will signal his arrival by coming down the Mount of Olives, crossing the Kidron Valley and entering the Temple through the eastern wall's Golden Gate. When Jesus followed this path riding a donkey, he was welcomed as the Messiah by followers waving palm branches. Rabbi Irving Greenberg famously said in 1967 that the difference between Jews and Christians will finally be settled when the Messiah descends the Mount of Olives and announces whether it his first or second trip.

To the left of the path modern visitors take down the Mount of Olives is an ancient cemetery, containing about 70,000 tombs from the time of King Solomon's Temple to the present. For thousands of years, Jews desiring a ring side seat for the Messiah's arrival have been interred along the Mount of Olives' western slope. Some believe, like other Jews and Christians, that the Messiah's appearance (first or second) will initiate the bodily resurrection of the dead. Consequently, they are buried with their feet to the east to be able to greet the Messiah face to face as they arise from their tombs. In the meantime, people pay their respects by placing small rocks on the stone tomb covers, reflecting their belief that the entombed souls are eternal.

A single grave site on the Mount of Olives reportedly costs up to $85,000. For those who can't afford to await the Messiah from there, there may be no reason to worry. An ancient legend says believers from around the world will be able to tunnel to the Mount of Olives when the Messiah arrives.

Where was Gabriel?

Cave beneath Basilica of the Annunciation in Nazareth, Israel

Every March 25, just after the vernal equinox and exactly nine months before Christmas, thousands of pilgrims visit Nazareth to remember the Annunciation, the time Christians believe the angel Gabriel revealed to Mary she would conceive the Son of God. Roman Catholics head for the Basilica of the Annunciation, the largest church in the Middle East. Greek Orthodox visitors go instead to the smaller Church of St. Gabriel. Each church claims to lie over the exact spot where Gabriel encountered Mary. Based on a writing unknown to most Christians, both churches may be right.

The Greek Orthodox Church of St. Gabriel lies over an ancient spring, visible below the church, which first became a church site early in the fourth century. The original church was built by Roman Emperor Constantine, apparently at the urging of one Count Joseph, who claimed Gabriel had spoken to Mary at the spring. Less than half a mile away, the Franciscan Basilica of the Annunciation lies above a cave claimed to have been the childhood home of Mary when Gabriel came calling. The first church on this site was built sometime after 383 A.D., when a Spanish nun named Lady Egeria visited Nazareth and returned saying that she had found the cave in which Mary lived. Today that cave is a grotto under the church, with stairs leading to a room claimed to be Mary's kitchen and a column marking the traditional spot where Gabriel stood while making his momentous announcement.

The *Gospel of Luke*, the only Biblical account of the Annunciation, says only that Gabriel came to Mary at "Nazareth, a town in Galilee." The *Infancy Gospel of James*, a popular second century text elaborating on the Biblical narratives about Mary, reports that Gabriel first approached Mary as she was fetching water for her jar and then completed his revelation in Mary's home, to which she had retreated, trembling with fear.

Visitors to Nazareth can refer to their copies of the *Infancy Gospel of James*, now available online, and conclude they could appropriately celebrate the Annunciation in both churches.

Away in a Manger

Stable under House in Taybeh, Palestinian Territories

Taybeh is a small Christian town on the West Bank, a few miles from Jerusalem. A Palestinian house discovered near a Taybeh church has changed the way that many people understand an important part of the traditional Christmas story. The pregnant mother of Jesus might not have been turned away by a heartless innkeeper after all.

The small house in Taybeh has two rooms. The larger room is where the owner's family cooks, eats and sleeps. An adjoining smaller room, accessible through a narrow door and up a couple of steps, allows visiting relatives some privacy. Under the house, in a cave carved in the limestone, is a stable where the family's few animals are kept. A feed trough or manger about the size of an infant lies along the stable's back wall.

So what does this house have to do with the Christmas story? Scholars believe the Taybeh house is similar to houses common in first century Judea. The Greek name for the upper guest room is "*kataluma*," the word that has been translated as "upper room" in English versions of *Gospel of Luke's* account of the Last Supper. English translators, having never seen a first century house, rendered the identical word "inn" in Luke's story of the birth of Jesus.

Looking at the Taybeh house, a growing number of scholars believe Luke reports that Jesus was born in a stable under the house of a relative, either because the *kataluma* upstairs was filled or, more likely, was not considered an appropriate place for a birth. This interpretation aligns with the ancient tradition that Jesus was born in a cave. An unavailable guest room also seems more likely than an overcrowded inn in first century Bethlehem, a town both too small and too close to Jerusalem to support such a facility.

Some Bible translations now use "guest room" instead of "inn" as the place lacking room for Jesus' birth. But when it comes to Bible stories, traditions often trump scholarship. Don't expect Christmas pageants to replace the innkeeper with a relative of Joseph gently leading Mary to the stable downstairs anytime soon.

The City on a Hill

Western Gate of Hippos, near Ein Gev, Israel

Since 1630, when Puritan leader John Winthrop addressed his followers onboard the ship *Arbella*, politicians have likened the American experience to the shining "city on a hill" described by Jesus in his Sermon on the Mount. They might have opted for a different metaphor if they had known that Jesus was referring to the glistening buildings of a thoroughly pagan city.

Jesus delivered his famous sermon from the northwestern shore of the Sea of Galilee, near his base in Capernaum. At the time, Hippos was a bustling city atop a flat hill rising more than 1000 feet above the water on the eastern shore of the lake, near today's Kibbutz Ein Gev. In making his points, Jesus referred to salt and lamps, items his followers encountered every day. Most scholars believe Jesus had Hippos in mind when he told his listeners that "a city that is set on a hill cannot be hidden" because it was the only hilltop city they had seen.

Hippos was founded by the Greeks in about 200 B.C., its name reflecting the hill's claimed resemblance to a horse. After a period under control of the Jewish Hasmoneans, in 63 B.C. the city came under control of the Romans, who made it one of the ten semi-autonomous Greco-Roman cities of the Decapolis. Recent excavations have revealed that life in first-century Hippos was much different from that in the Jewish fishing villages where Jesus usually taught. Archaeologists have uncovered a column-lined Roman main street running the 500-meter length of the hilltop, flanked by theaters, temples to Zeus and Aphrodite, and a fountain dedicated to sensuous water nymphs, all gleaming in the afternoon sun when Jesus and his followers gazed across the lake.

A narrow path leads to the ruins of Hippos, with signs warning: "Mines on both sides of the trail; walk only on the marked path." At the top of the hill are remains of several Byzantine-era churches, destroyed by an earthquake in 749 A.D. Hundreds of years after the Sermon on the Mount, Christian lights finally shone from the famous city on a hill.

When Pigs Flew

Sea of Galilee from Gadara, Jordan

In one of the stranger stories in the Christian *New Testament,* Jesus drove evil spirits from a man so tormented by them that not even chains could restrain him. The evil spirits then went into 2000 pigs, causing them to rush down a steep bank into the lake below, where they all drowned. Although the Bible does not unambiguously indicate where this story took place, the most likely spot is near the well-excavated ruins of Gadara in extreme northwestern Jordan, 2000 feet above the Sea of Galilee.

Gadara was one of ten Greco-Roman cities constituting the Decapolis. Like life in other Decapolis cities, first century life in Gadara was much different from life in the Jewish areas nearby. Citizens attended the now reconstructed theater and shopped along the colonnaded main street that still shows the ruts formed by Roman chariot wheels. Men bathed in the nude in the pubic baths. And, of course, unlike their Jewish neighbors, the residents of Gadara ate plenty of pork, which explains why so many pigs were nearby when Jesus drove the demons from the man they were tormenting.

According to the Bible, the man Jesus cured of his demons was so happy to be able to live a normal life that he went into the Decapolis, spreading his good news. The first Decapolis city he reached was probably Hippos. Traveling a few miles south, the man from Gadara would have come to Scythopolis, the capital of the Decapolis. Visitors today can explore its meticulously restored theater, baths and temples, as well as the nearby excavation of Beth She'an, where the victorious Philistines hung the headless body of Saul, Israel's first king.

On a clear day in Gadara, it is possible to see Jordan, Syria, Israel and Lebanon. It is also possible to imagine Jesus and his Jewish followers crossing the Sea of Galilee from their base in Capernaum, climbing the steep hill to Gadara's alien culture and, without preconditions, helping a man holding religious beliefs far different from their own. There are lessons for all of us in Gadara.

The Garden
and Gethsemane

Traditional "Garden of Gethsemane" in Jerusalem

Every year during Passion Week, Christians around the world rehear the story of Jesus' agony in the Garden of Gethsemane. Travelers to Jerusalem can visit what is said to be the very garden. But whether Jesus ever set foot in that garden is far from certain.

Surprising to many Christians, the Bible never mentions a Garden of Gethsemane. The *Gospels of Mark* and *Matthew* report that Jesus shared a Passover meal with his disciples before going to "Gethsemane," a corruption of Hebrew words literally meaning "wine press for oils," where he prayed and was then betrayed by Judas. The *Gospel of John* says Jesus prayed with his disciples the night before Passover and was later betrayed by Judas in an unnamed "garden." From these accounts, some Christians concluded that Gethsemane was a garden, while others concluded Jesus prayed at the site of a wine press and then went to a garden.

Since the fourth century, Christians have identified multiple locations near the foot of the Mount of Olives matching their own conceptions of Gethsemane. The most popular site is a walled garden across the Kidron Valley from the Temple Mount. It includes flower-lined paths and eight olive trees carbon dated to the time of the Crusaders, making them the oldest such trees on Earth. The adjoining Church of All Nations, built in the 1920s on the site of earlier churches, is claimed to cover the stone on which Jesus knelt while he prayed. At least three other locations on the Mount of Olives, including a cave said to have housed an ancient wine press, are also associated with the Biblical accounts of Jesus' agony in Gethsemane. The traditional choices for Gethsemane are all near major first century roads crossing the Mount of Olives. Some scholars believe a secluded location north and east of traditional locations would be a more likely spot for someone seeking to pray.

For Christian visitors to Jerusalem, whether the traditional sites of Gethsemane are precisely the place of Jesus' agony is irrelevant. Being in the vicinity of where Jesus prayed on the night before his crucifixion is close enough.

The Rolling Stone

The Garden Tomb in Jerusalem

Each spring, thousands of Christians make a pilgrimage to the tomb of Jesus in Jerusalem, many having a powerful spiritual experience. Surprisingly, they have a choice of tombs and the one they pick may depend on their beliefs.

The first choice was located by Helena, who, at age 80, was sent to the Holy Land by her son, Emperor Constantine, to find sites important to Christianity. She returned in 328 A.D. with news she had found the tomb of Jesus in Jerusalem. The Church of the Holy Sepulchre was soon built around the tomb. So, for almost 1700 years Christians have made their way to that now cavernous church.

After the Reformation, Protestants began looking for another tomb, at least in part because of their discomfort in worshipping in the all-too-Catholic Church of the Holy Sepulchre. Protestants were therefore thrilled in 1883 when English General Charles Gordon found a tomb near a Jerusalem rock formation suggesting a skull, which he thought identified the Biblical Golgotha where Jesus had been crucified. For General Gordon, the clincher was a groove on the ground that he thought had been used to roll a stone across the opening. And so, with great fanfare, the Garden Tomb opened to the public. Protestants came in large numbers to what they also called Gordon's Calvary.

In 1986, Israeli archaeologist Gabriel Barkay, an authority on Jewish tombs, published an article concluding that the Garden Tomb was not used at the time of Jesus. He also made a simple observation that had escaped General Gordon. The groove in front of the tomb sloped away from the opening and would have prevented the tomb from being closed by a rolling stone. The groove was probably a trough for watering animals, added by the Crusaders who used the tomb as a stable.

Guides at the Garden Tomb no longer claim it held the body of Jesus. But Protestant visitors still worship there, experiencing the same emotions as before. Others continue to experience comparable emotions at the Church of the Holy Sepulchre. As with many other sites in the Holy Land, tradition and belief can be as important as archaeology.

Temple to a
Forgotten God

Perimeter Wall of Temple of Ba'al in Palmyra, Syria

About 150 miles northeast of Damascus are the partially reconstructed ruins of the ancient city of Palmyra. Those ruins include what has been described as the most important religious building in the Middle East during the first century, a building that mimics the Second Temple in Jerusalem with one very important difference.

Palmyra was founded near a fertile oasis in the middle of the Syrian Desert in about 2000 B.C. It began to prosper as caravans traveling between the Far East and the Mediterranean stopped for water and supplies. The residents were only too willing to accommodate the travelers if the price was right. By the first century, Palmyra had become one of the wealthiest cities in the Middle East, its wealth reflected by a magnificent theater and a main street flanked by 1500 Corinthian columns.

Many people come to Palmyra to see a huge temple complex, occupying nearly an acre, built in 32 A.D. to honor Ba'al, the Canaanite god of war and weather. That complex, with its Holy of Holies or *cella* and its altar of undressed stone, is remarkably similar to descriptions of the Jewish Second Temple, destroyed by the Romans in 70 A.D. It seems likely that the temple to Ba'al was influenced by the temple in Jerusalem. But there was one very important difference. The Palmyra temple included a statue of Ba'al in its Holy of Holies, while the Holy of Holies in Jerusalem was occupied only by the spirit of the transcendent Yahweh.

West of the temple to Ba'al are the famous tower tombs, unique to Palmyra. Families placed their dead and their possessions in morgue-like compartments in these multi-story towers and then sealed the opening with a slab of stone carved in relief to reflect the life of the deceased.

Some of the ruins in Palmyra, a UNESCO World Heritage site, have been intentionally destroyed during the Syrian civil war. Physical evidence helping to visualize the Temple in Jerusalem may be lost forever. But what cannot be lost is the understanding that Ba'al has long since been forgotten and the God worshipped in Jerusalem is still worshipped around the world.

Where Christians
Became Christians

Cave Church in Antakya, Turkey

A small cave in the mountainside above the city of Antakya in southern Turkey may well be the oldest church in the world, dating to the earliest days of Christianity. It was also in or near this cave that early Christians argued over a matter that proved crucial to the ultimate success of Christianity.

In the first century, Antakya, then known as Antioch, was the third largest city in the world. According to the Bible, Paul and Barnabas spent a year in Antioch recruiting new followers of Jesus, where those followers were first called Christians. Exactly where in Antioch those early Christians may have met is impossible to determine, but a natural cave on the side of Mount Starius has long been thought to be that place. Not everything in the cave goes back to the time of Paul and Barnabas. But a watery hole in the cave floor long used for baptisms may have existed in the first century and a narrow passage to the outside might have been used by early Christians to escape the Romans.

While in Antioch, Paul taught that circumcision was not necessary for Gentiles who wanted to follow Jesus. James, the brother of Jesus and the leader of the church in Jerusalem, disagreed and sent a delegation to Antioch to try to convince Paul that he was wrong. Paul eventually won the argument. With the requirement of circumcision no longer an impediment to gaining non-Jewish followers, Paul set off from Antioch on the missionary journeys that eventually spread Christianity to the far reaches of the Roman Empire.

Roman Catholics have identified Peter as the first bishop of Antioch, which became an important city in the early church. So the cave church in Antioch, although founded by Paul and Barnabas, is now named for Peter.

Many sites traditionally associated with early events in Christian history are suspect at best. But the cave in Antakya has sufficient indicia of authenticity that it may legitimately be considered the place where Paul broke Christianity away from its Jewish moorings to become a religion of the Gentiles.

Believe it or Not

Main Street in Ephesus, Turkey

Ephesus was one of the Roman Empire's most important and sophisticated cities, with a population of up to 500,000 and a beautiful library housing more than 12,000 scrolls. Completely abandoned in the fifteenth century, the city near modern Izmir is now among Turkey's most important tourist destinations. Many visitors seek the sites of historical religious controversies and controversial religious histories.

First century Ephesians worshipped the fertility goddess Artemis, whose temple was one of the seven wonders of the ancient world. According to the *Book of Acts*, when the Apostle Paul told Ephesians their silver idols of Artemis were not real gods, silversmiths touched off a riot in the 25,000-seat Great Theater, then the largest in the world. The Great Theater is still largely intact, but the famous temple to Artemis was demolished by a Christian mob in 401 A.D.

Early Christians believed that John, the beloved disciple of Jesus, lived and was buried near Ephesus, so Roman (Byzantine) Emperor Justinian I built a magnificent basilica over the claimed grave site in the sixth century. Jesus' mother Mary also lived in Ephesus, or so the story goes, because Jesus tasked John with looking after her just before he died on the cross. Visitors to Ephesus climb a steep hill to a brick house where a German seer said Mary lived, many wondering why the house looks so recently built. Reflecting the importance of both Jesus and Mary to Muslims, the fourteenth century Isa (Jesus) Bey Mosque was built within sight of the basilica of St. John.

In about 450 A.D., an influential bishop reported that seven young Christian men had fallen asleep in a cave near Ephesus while avoiding Roman persecution and awoke about two hundred years later, amazed that the Empire was now Christian. The Quran reports essentially the same story, the most significant difference being that a dog stayed awake to guard the cave. A grotto near Ephesus honors the "Seven Sleepers of Ephesus."

Which of the religious claims for Ephesus are real is largely a matter of belief. But what is undoubtedly real is the powerful experience of visiting a city that has inspired so many beliefs.

Gods and Politics

Athens Agora, with Mars Hill on the Right

The colonnaded Parthenon atop the flat hill of the Athenian Acropolis is one of the most recognizable structures in the world, epitomizing Classical architecture. But the buildings below the Acropolis were more important to the history of both democracy and Christianity.

As early as the seventh century B.C., the lower area northwest of the Acropolis was cleared of houses and reserved for use as an agora (marketplace). After the Greeks defeated the Persians in 480 B.C., Athens became the most important city in Greece and the agora became the center of Athenian life. The agora included buildings where citizens enacted legislation and served as jurors in law cases. It also included temples and monuments to Athens' pantheon of gods and goddesses, including Apollo, Hephaestus and Aphrodite. The so-called "Altar of the Twelve Gods" established the point from which all distances in Athens were measured. A stone inscription referenced an "unknown god," reportedly responsible for a devastating plague. West of the Acropolis a marble outcropping known as Mars Hill held the Areopagus, an institution performing various governmental functions over time.

When the Romans conquered Athens in about 88 B.C., they largely retained the buildings and temples of the agora. In the first century, people gathered in the Areopagus to discuss philosophical and political matters. According to the *Book of Acts*, when Paul visited Athens in about 51 A.D., he was distressed by all the idols he saw being worshipped in the temples. After seeking to make followers of Jesus among people walking about the agora, Paul debated Athenian intellectuals in the Areopagus. He argued that the transcendent God of the Jews was the unknown god they had been seeking. A few influential Athenians reportedly accepted Paul's argument and became Christians.

The Athens agora has been maintained as a public site and some of its buildings are remarkably well preserved. A plaque at the base of Mars Hill displays the argument Paul made to the Areopagus, reflecting Christianity's current status as the state religion of Greece. The precise identities of the Twelve Gods, once worshipped at the center of Athens, are long forgotten.

Treasure Map
or Ancient Hoax?

Portion of Copper Scroll at Jordan Archaeological Museum

The so-called "Copper Scroll," now housed in a Jordanian museum, identifies hidden caches of almost unimaginable quantities of gold and silver. Although some scholars believe the scroll is a 2000-year-old hoax, would-be Indiana Joneses keep digging.

After local Bedouins found the original Dead Sea Scrolls in caves near Jericho in 1946, archaeologists searched 250 nearby caves. In 1952, they found two scrolls in what became known as Cave 3, made of high-grade copper instead of the parchment and papyrus of scrolls found earlier. Because the metal had long since corroded and become brittle, the scrolls could not be unrolled. A laboratory in Manchester, England, eventually opened the scrolls by cutting them lengthwise and then separating the sheets. The translated Hebrew text, written in script unlike that of the other scrolls, showed the two scrolls were part of a single scroll that had separated before being rolled. What became known as the Copper Scroll lists 64 locations where specified quantities of gold, silver and other treasures can be found. Some experts have estimated the total amount of gold and silver to be more than five million ounces, worth billions of dollars at current prices.

Scholars are divided about who made the Copper Scroll and what, if any, treasures it describes. Some believe the scroll identifies items from the Second Temple in Jerusalem, hidden before the Temple was destroyed by the Romans in 70 A.D. Others argue the items were accumulated by first century Essenes living in Qumran, near where the scroll was found. Still others claim the treasures came from the First Temple, destroyed by the Babylonians in 586 B.C. Finally, some scholars believe the Copper Scroll repeated an ancient fable. Fable or not, explorers from around the world have sought fame and fortune using the ambiguous descriptions in the Copper Scroll, so far digging up only dirt.

Because Jordan financed the expedition that found the Copper Scroll, for years it was displayed in the Jordanian Archaeological Museum. The scroll recently moved to a much larger display in the newly opened Jordan Museum in Amman, where it is among the museum's most popular items.

Mountain Top Experiences

Masada, near the Dead Sea in Israel

For Herod the Great, the king of Judea at the time of the birth of Jesus, Masada was a place to keep cool in the summer. For the people of modern Israel, Masada is a constant reminder of the courage of their ancestors and a symbol of their own determination.

During his reign from about 36 to 4 B.C., Herod was one of the most prodigious builders of his era, trying to improve the image of his little kingdom in the eyes of his bosses in Rome. The accomplishments of Herod's engineers were remarkable. But none of Herod's many building projects have had the lasting psychological influence of Masada, rising 1300 feet above the Judean desert. At the top of this rocky plateau, Herod built an elaborate city, complete with Roman baths, an underground reservoir holding a million gallons of water and a three tier summer palace overlooking the Dead Sea. The only way up to the fortified complex was along a narrow "snake path."

In 66 A.D., Jewish revolutionaries captured Masada from the Romans. They and the families that joined them held out against a Roman siege for seven years until engineers built an earthen ramp to the top and soldiers broke down the walls. Both the site of the Roman encampment and the remains of the ramp can still be seen from the snake path. According to Josephus, the first-century Jewish historian, the entering Roman soldiers found all but seven of the 960 holdouts dead, killed by their own hands to avoid being taken alive.

Today, a metal plaque at Masada, a UNESCO World Heritage site, reads: "What of us? What is our Masada? How much of all this will we take with us, and how much of our own will we add?" Since the time of Moshe Dayan, new members of the Israeli military have walked up the snake path for a torch-lit swearing-in ceremony among the ruins, which ends with a pledge that "Masada shall not fall again." For everyone visiting Masada, the mountain top, now also reachable by cable car, is a powerful reminder of the indomitable Jewish spirit and the universal yearning of people to be free.

The Menorah
in the Roman Arch

Arch of Titus in Rome, Italy

Lying between the ruins of the Roman Forum and the Coliseum is a monument celebrating the destruction of the Second Temple in Jerusalem. Ironically, this same monument provided the model for the emblem of modern Israel.

The Second Temple was one of the most impressive buildings in the Middle East during the early part of the first century. Substantially enhanced by Herod the Great to burnish his own image, the Temple displayed a large seven-candle menorah, fashioned of solid gold according to a design the Bible says God gave Moses. In 66 A.D., a minor protest against Roman rule got out of hand and led to the First Jewish Revolt. Emperor Nero sent 60,000 troops to Judea with instructions to crush it. Four years later, after a long siege, Roman soldiers under the command of Titus broke through the walls of Jerusalem, slaughtered the residents and destroyed the Second Temple.

Titus, who later became emperor, was honored in 82 A.D. with a 50-foot-high marble arch near the Forum memorializing the success of his campaign against Judea. The inside wall of the arch contains a carved relief showing Roman troops hauling items looted from the Second Temple, including the menorah, trumpets and a sacred table. Recent scientific analysis has confirmed that a layer of gold originally covered the plunder shown in the relief.

In 1949, the leaders of Israel decided that the emblem of their new country should depict the seven-candle menorah, a symbol of Judaism for thousands of years. But the menorah taken from the Second Temple was destroyed in antiquity. The best evidence of what it had looked like was the relief inside the Arch of Titus. So designers used that relief as the model for the menorah now at the center of Israel's official emblem.

Most visitors to the Roman Forum scurry past the Arch of Titus on their way to the Coliseum. The next time you are in Rome, look inside the arch for the menorah that not only became the symbol of Israel but confirms the golden splendor of the Second Temple.

No Christians Died Here

Coliseum and Arch of Titus in Rome, Italy

Millions visit the Roman Coliseum every year, many of them expecting to see where Christians were thrown to hungry lions. But Coliseum guides quickly dash those expectations, pointing out that facts don't support the gory images of Renaissance paintings and late night movies.

Roman Emperor Vespasian ordered construction of the Coliseum in 72 A.D. The nearby Arch of Titus, erected at about the same time, shows Roman troops under Vespasian's son Titus bringing golden treasures looted from the Jewish Second Temple back to Rome. Scholars believe these treasures funded the building of the Coliseum. Titus also brought back to Rome 20,000 Jewish slaves, many of whom were forced to build the Coliseum. When completed in 80 A.D., the Coliseum was a powerful reminder of the public benefits of Roman military power.

The four-tier oval Coliseum included numbered seats for at least 57,000 spectators and a long-gone retractable cover. Coliseum entertainment typically involved fighting and death. During the inaugural games, 9000 animals from around the Empire were reportedly killed. Gladiators, both prisoners seeking freedom and professionals seeking glory, fought to the death unless the "Editor," often the Emperor, granted them mercy.

What about the Christians and the lions? Some evidence suggests that Romans executed early Christians by exposing them to dogs or other unspecified "wild beasts." The tradition that the beasts were lions was probably influenced by the Biblical story of Daniel and the lions' den. But scholars have found no reliable evidence linking Christian deaths of any kind to the Coliseum. The first hint of a connection came in the sixteenth century, when Pope Pius V suggested to Christian pilgrims in Rome that sand from the Coliseum floor contained the blood of martyrs and could be taken home as a holy relic.

When visiting the Coliseum, don't expect to see where the lions ate the Christians. Instead, expect to get an understanding of the horror first century Jews experienced when treasures of their holy Temple were used to construct a pagan monument to fighting and death. Even today, the Talmud forbids Jews from walking under Titus' humiliating arch.

Where Everyone
Got Along

Ruins of Synagogue at Dura Europos, Syria

The last place most people would expect to find evidence of religious tolerance is near the Syrian border with Iraq. But that is exactly where it can be found.

Macedonian Greeks built Dura Europos in 303 B.C. atop a steep cliff 300 feet above the west bank of the Euphrates River. Despite its natural protections, the city fell to the Persians in 113 B.C. Romans then conquered the city in about 160 A.D., making it a base for their military and commercial operations along the Euphrates. The Roman army and immigrants brought religious beliefs and languages from around the Empire to Dura Europos, making it an early melting pot. In about 256 A.D. Persians again captured the city and deported its residents. Earthen embankments built in an unsuccessful attempt to protect the city collapsed, covering some of the buildings. Sand and mud eventually covered the rest and the city remained hidden for hundreds of years.

Archaeologists began uncovering Dura Europos in 1920 after the British army stumbled onto some ancient paintings. What the archaeologists found was comparable to Pompeii. The sand and mud had stopped time in the third century. Well-preserved wall paintings, now in museums in Syria and the United States, enabled identification of the original purpose of many buildings. A house built in about 235 A.D. was used as a church, with a painting of Jesus and Peter walking on water the oldest surviving representation of Jesus. Its baptistery is the oldest one in the world. A large synagogue with 28 colorful paintings of Biblical scenes was dated to about 240 A.D., making it the oldest known synagogue outside Israel. Sixteen temples and a Mithraeum honored Greek, Roman, Persian and Canaanite gods.

During the third century, as Christians were being persecuted in Rome, worshippers in the house-church in Dura Europos lived peaceably amid temples to Adonis, Artemis and Ba'al. As anti-Semitism was poisoning relations between Christians and Jews elsewhere, an impressive synagogue was being built near the church. We can all learn about interfaith tolerance and cooperation from ancient ruins near the Euphrates River.

Churches and
Fairy Chimneys

Fairy Chimneys at Cappadocia, Turkey

Describing the surreal landscape of Cappadocia is probably the only time the words "fairy" and "church" can be used respectfully in the same sentence. In this region in central Turkey, fairy chimneys can become churches, tunnels can become cities and the incomprehensible can become settled theology.

Cappadocia lies north of the Taurus Mountains, where a series of volcanic eruptions produced a plateau made of thick lava layers. Water and wind then eroded the lava, producing thousands of cone-shaped structures called fairy chimneys, some more than 120 feet tall and a few balancing hard caps on their improbably pointed peaks. For millennia, residents of Cappadocia have hollowed out the soft lava of the fairy chimneys to create homes resembling stone tepees, the porosity of the lava providing excellent insulation. After Christianity had come to Cappadocia through the missionary visits of Paul, the interiors of fairy chimneys became churches.

The soft lava of Cappadocia also facilitated the expansion of tunnels into at least 36 full-blown underground cities, some extending ten stories below the surface. Originally used by the Hittites almost 4000 years ago, these cities were occupied by early Christians, perhaps to hide from Roman persecutors.

After Christianity became legal, Cappadocians helped resolve a theological controversy. When the Council of Nicaea in 325 A.D. decreed that God and Jesus were of the same substance [*homoousios*], many Christians objected, arguing that God and Jesus were obviously different. Theologians from Cappadocia, trained in Greek philosophy and called the Cappadocian Fathers, taught that things having the same substance can also have different expressions [*hypostases*], pointing to gold coins made from the same ingot but having faces of different persons. This conception of God in three persons, ratified by the Council of Constantinople in 381 A.D., ended the argument for many Christians.

Today's visitors to Cappadocia, a UNESCO World Heritage site, can tour underground cities with kitchens still black from cooking smoke and admire brilliantly colored tenth century frescoes in dark churches. And people for whom the Holy Trinity is important can thank the Cappadocian Fathers for at least trying to make it more understandable.

Another Bethlehem Cave

Saints Eustochium, Paula, Jerome and Eusebius of Cremona in Bethlehem Cave

Christians all over the world travel to Bethlehem each year at Christmastime to see the cave below the Church of the Nativity where tradition says Jesus was born. Another Bethlehem cave honors the man who created a translation of the Nativity story that remained unchanged for almost 1600 years.

Saint Jerome was born in about 342 A.D. and studied Latin and Greek in Rome. Rejecting what he considered the depravity of Roman life, he converted to Christianity, studied theology and traveled to churches around the Empire, eventually becoming a priest. In 382 A.D., Pope Damasus asked Jerome, then back in Rome, to make a definitive Latin translation of the four Gospels from their original Greek. While completing his assignment, Jerome aroused suspicion because of his close relationship with a wealthy Roman widow named Paula and her daughter Eustochium. The three moved to Bethlehem, where Paula and Eustochium established monasteries and convents. They also supported and assisted the ascetic Jerome as he worked alone in a tiny cave for 34 years, translating most of the remainder of the Bible into Latin from the original Hebrew and Greek.

Jerome's life's work, the "vulgate" or "common" translation, became the standard Bible of Roman Catholics until the twentieth century, but it was not error free. His mistaken translation of the Hebrew word meaning "radiant" as "horned" led artists, including Michelangelo, to depict Moses with horns on his head.

The cave where Jerome labored is now a chapel beneath Bethlehem's Church of St. Catherine of Alexandria. Wall mosaics depict Eustochium, Paula, Jerome and Eusebius of Cremona, who managed the monasteries after Jerome's death. All became saints, with Paula considered the patron saint of widows, and all were buried in an adjacent cave. Jerome's remains were later moved to Rome and parts of his body are claimed by several churches. A statue outside the church depicts Jerome with a human skull at his feet, his constant reminder of the shortness of life.

Every visit to Bethlehem begins with a visit to the cave of Jesus' birth. It should end with a visit to the cave of Saint Jerome.

World's Pole
Sitting Record

Ruins of Church of St. Simeon the Stylite, near Aleppo, Syria

One of the world's oldest churches honors a fifth century ascetic whose record for endurance has remained unbroken. The church itself originated a design that is still emulated.

The person known as Simeon the Stylite was born to a Christian shepherd family near the southern border of Turkey in about 388 A.D. At age 13, he heard a sermon about the Beatitudes and decided to devote his life to sacrifice. Simeon joined a monastery as a teenager, but was asked to leave because of his extreme asceticism, which included tying a rope around his body so tightly that the flesh died. After departing the monastery, he went for 40 days during Lent without eating or drinking. On other occasions, he reportedly stood during the entire Lenten period.

As Simeon's reputation for self-denial spread, people flocked to him, seeking prayers and advice. He fled to a remote mountain top near Aleppo, Syria, to avoid the crowds. When admirers followed him, he got away from them vertically by living on a meter-square platform atop a nine-foot-high pillar (Greek *stylos*). As curious crowds gathered in larger numbers, Simeon extended the pillar until the platform, from which he never descended, was about 50-feet above the ground. He preached daily to the people below and occasionally wrote letters to his followers. Even emperors sought his counsel.

Simeon died while praying in 459 A.D., having spent 37 years on his pillar. He was soon named a saint and honored with the oldest surviving Byzantine church, enclosing about 53,000 square feet. Four basilicas, oriented in the cardinal directions, formed a cross and surrounded an octagonal court that encompassed Simeon's famous pillar.

Following the example of Simeon, other ascetics began living on pillars, becoming known as stylites. Alfred, Lord Tennyson memorialized Simeon the Stylite in an 1833 poem and the *Guinness Book of World Records* gives him the world's record for pole sitting, its longest unbroken record. The ruins of the Church of St. Simeon the Stylite, with only the base of his famous pillar surviving, are a UNESCO World Heritage site, which have so far survived the fighting in Syria.

Did St. George
Save His Church?

Church of St. George in Ezra, Syria

In 2015, members of a small church in Ezra, Syria, celebrated 1500 years of worshipping God in the same building. Some attribute this extraordinary longevity to the contents of a special box.

Ezra lies about 50 miles south of Damascus along the western edge of the Hauran, a fertile plateau that played a role in the early development of agriculture. Today, Ezra is best known for its domed Church of St. George. The square building is made of basaltic rock and includes two inscribed octagonal structures, the inner one supporting the dome. An inscription between two crosses over the door says the Greek Orthodox Church was erected in 515 A.D. on the site of a pagan temple. Except for a nineteenth century reconstruction of its damaged dome, the building remains essentially unchanged since its erection.

Colorful icons and gold vigil lamps adorn the sanctuary, but the church's most prized possession is a box, draped with a rich red cloth, resting behind the altar. A stone plaque leaning against the base of the box bears the iconic image of St. George killing a dragon. The inscription above the entrance says the church was built to house the remains of St. George. Church members believe remains of the martyred St. George are in the box. How much remains of him is not so clear. A sarcophagus in the Church of St. George in Lod (Lydda), Israel, considered the birthplace of St. George, is said to hold his body. His head has been claimed by churches in both Greece and Italy.

The Ezra church has a distinction none of the other sites claiming St. George's remains can match – it is one of the oldest continuously functioning church buildings in the world. Some attribute the church's long survival to the admiration Syrian Muslims also have for St. George, the patron saint of not only England and Georgia but Palestine and Egypt. Members of Ezra's Church of St. George look instead to their draped box, topped with tokens of gratitude. For them, St. George has protected this ancient house of worship.

Recorded History

Hagia Sophia in Istanbul, Turkey

Istanbul's Hagia Sophia is one of the world's most intriguing buildings. Its dome is a marvel of sixth century engineering and its icons are a visible record of the area's still tumultuous religious history.

In 527 A.D., with the Western Roman Empire in collapse, Justinian I became the Eastern (Byzantine) Emperor in Constantinople, founded by Emperor Constantine. When a rebellion destroyed a small Constantinople church named Hagia Sophia (Holy Wisdom), Justinian ordered a new church built on its site. Ten thousand workers spent six years building a new Hagia Sophia to reflect Justinian's dream of returning the Empire to its former glory. Luxurious materials, including marble columns from the temple to Artemis at Ephesus, came from throughout the Empire. A 100-foot-diameter dome was supported on 40 arched windows ingeniously resting on a square base. Icons helped illiterate worshippers understand Biblical teachings. When completed in 537 A.D., Hagia Sophia became the seat of the Archbishop (Patriarch) of Constantinople.

In 726 A.D., Emperor Leo III, likely influenced by Islamic beliefs, ordered the destruction of Hagia Sophia's icons as forbidden graven images. The icons were restored in 843 A.D., when Emperor Michael III repudiated the iconoclasts. In 1054, the Archbishop of Rome sent an emissary to the Hagia Sophia to excommunicate the Archbishop of Constantinople, dividing Christians between Roman Catholics and Eastern Orthodox. Crusaders sent east by Catholic kings captured Constantinople in 1204 and carried icons and relics looted from Hagia Sophia back to Venice. In 1261, Byzantine forces recaptured Hagia Sophia and added golden icons incorporating a style still common in Eastern Orthodox churches.

Muslims under Mehmed II captured Constantinople from the Byzantines in 1453, renamed the city Istanbul and converted Hagia Sophia, at the time the largest church in the world, into a mosque. The icons were again covered, four minarets were added and a golden *mihrab* marked the direction of Mecca.

After the Islamic Ottoman Empire was defeated in World War I, Hagia Sophia came under control of the Republic of Turkey, which uncovered the icons and made Hagia Sophia a museum. Some Turks insist that Hagia Sophia should again be a mosque, with the icons again covered. Stay tuned.

An Underground Forest

Basilica Cistern in Istanbul, Turkey

After the Western Roman Empire had collapsed in the late fifth century, the Eastern (Byzantine) Empire remained a center of culture and learning. Eastern Emperor Justinian I added to the grandeur of his capital in Constantinople, now called Istanbul. The magnificent church of Hagia Sophia was only one of many enduring achievements of Justinian's reign. Another was an underground reservoir built to supply water to what was then the world's largest city, with a population of 500,000.

Reportedly built by 7000 slaves, the Basilica Cistern, named for its location under the Stoa Basilica, is 453 feet long and 212 feet wide. Its 30-foot-high ceiling is supported by 336 marble and granite columns arranged in 12 rows of 28, with each group of four columns supporting an arched cross vault. With 13-foot-thick brick walls covered with water-resistant mortar, the reservoir could store more than 21 million gallons of water. The water, transported via aqueduct from a forest near the Black Sea, was distributed to Constantinople palaces and other buildings through a series of pipes.

The varying capital styles suggest that the columns were spoliated from pagan temples around the Empire. Two columns in the northwest corner are supported on stone pedestals bearing the carved image of snake-haired Medusa, one upside down and one on its side. Some believe these orientations were intended to cancel out the effects of Medusa's petrifying gaze, but exactly why such mythological features were placed in a structure commissioned by a Christian emperor remains a mystery. Another column bears an image of eyes and tears, said to memorialize the slaves who died during construction.

The Basilica Cistern was rediscovered in 1545 when people in Istanbul were observed fishing though holes in the ground. Today, 52 steps a few hundred feet from Hagia Sophia lead down to a clean and lighted forest of columns, used for concerts and as a location for *From Russia with Love*. When you are in Istanbul, stop by the Basilica Cistern to see one of the reasons why history calls the emperor who ordered its construction Justinian the Great.

This Way to the Church

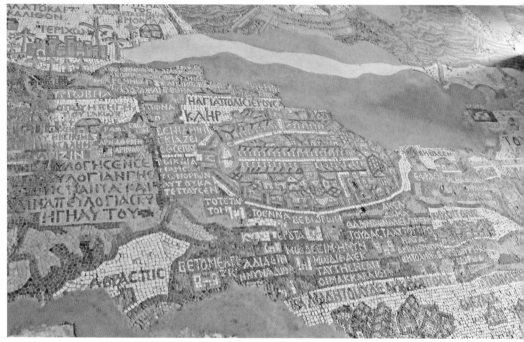

Map in Church of St. George in Madaba, Jordan

Most visitors to Madaba, a small city near Mt. Nebo in northwestern Jordan, come just to see a floor. That famous floor guided both sixth century Christian pilgrims and twentieth century archaeologists to one of the largest churches of antiquity.

In about 1896, the builders of Madaba's Church of St. George uncovered the floor of a Byzantine church built on the same site. The damaged floor included the remains of a large mosaic map of the area from Lebanon to the Nile Delta and from the Mediterranean to the eastern wilderness. The map, originally comprising about two million tiles, dates from about 570 A.D. and gave visitors to the Holy Land a visual understanding of the location of important Christian sites. It is the oldest known map of the area.

The map, with east at the top, identifies major locations in Greek. Near the center is an oversized representation of Jerusalem, bisected by a colonnaded cardo. In the middle of the cardo is the domed Church of the Holy Sepulchre, shown upside down with a red roof. Another church, with a slightly larger roof, is shown upright in the south (right) end of the cardo.

When the Madaba map was discovered, scholars assumed the church at the end of the cardo was the Nea Church, known from ancient records to have been built by Emperor Justinian I in about 542 A.D. and reported to have been the largest church in Jerusalem at the time. But the church itself had never been found. After the capture of the Jewish Quarter of Jerusalem by Israel in 1967, archaeologists from the Hebrew University of Jerusalem, using the Madaba map as their guide, found the ruins of the Nea Church and the adjacent cardo about 12 feet below the current street level. Measurements showed that the Nea Church covered almost two acres, nearly twice the size of the Hagia Sophia in Constantinople.

Today's visitors to Jerusalem can walk along the columns of the Roman cardo to the ruins of the Nea Church. Like their sixth century predecessors, they can thank the Madaba map makers for showing the way.

Saved by Wise Men

Church of the Nativity in Bethlehem, Palestinian Territories

Bethlehem's Church of the Nativity, celebrating the birth of Jesus, is believed to be the oldest complete church in the world. It may owe its extraordinary longevity to the power of the Biblical wise men from the east.

After Roman Emperor Constantine had accepted Christianity, he sent his already-Christian mother, Helena, to the Holy Land to find important Christian sites. She claimed to have found in Bethlehem the cave in which Jesus had been born, at the time covered by a temple to Adonis, the lover of Venus. Under orders from Rome, the temple was razed and replaced by a church in about 339 A.D. After the original church was destroyed during a revolt by Jews and Samaritans against the Byzantine Empire, Emperor Justinian I rebuilt the church in essentially its current form in 565 A.D., with two rows of columns on each side of a long main floor. A fourteen-point silver star in a basement cave marks the traditional spot of Jesus' birth.

When the Persians invaded what is now Israel in 614 A.D., they destroyed all the churches they could find. However, at least according to legend, they spared the Church of the Nativity because they concluded the wise men pictured inside were Persians and could not destroy a tribute to their countrymen.

The Crusaders refurbished the church's interior, but an early mosaic floor can still be seen through an opening in the current floor. In the 1500s, the height of the main door was lowered to less than four feet, reportedly to prevent people from riding their horses into the sanctuary. Today, people stand in line to squeeze through the tiny door.

Greek Orthodox and Armenian Christians control most of the Church of the Nativity, now a UNESCO World Heritage Site. Since they celebrate Christmas on January 7 and 19, respectively, the famous Christmas Eve service held in Bethlehem every December 24 is held in the nearby Roman Catholic Church of St. Catherine of Alexandria.

Sun Worship

Pyramid of the Sun at Teotihuacan, near Mexico City, Mexico

For anyone with an insatiable desire to see ancient pyramids and for whom a trip to Egypt is out of the question, a trip to Mexico offers an ideal solution. Just a few miles from Mexico City are the monumental pyramids of Teotihuacan, one of the world's most important cities during the first millennium.

Teotihuacan was founded as a religious center on a highlands plateau in about 200 B.C. By 600 A.D., Teotihuacan had a population of up to 200,000, making it the largest city in what are now the Americas and the sixth largest city in the world, about a third the size of Constantinople. Multi-story apartment buildings accommodated the large urban population, which included skilled potters and artists whose remarkably well preserved murals are still on display.

Teotihuacan's brick and stone pyramids are connected by a broad boulevard. The Pyramid of the Sun, constructed in about 100 A.D. along the boulevard, is the third largest pyramid in the world. At 733 feet per side, its base is about the size of that of the Great Pyramid of Giza but it rises only half as high. The Pyramids of the Moon and of the Feathered Serpent, at opposite ends of the boulevard, are smaller but equally impressive. The pyramids of Teotihuacan were built as places of worship, with temples to influential gods on their flattened summits. Bodies buried in the pyramids with their hands tied have been interpreted as sacrifices to those gods, probably made at the times the temples were dedicated.

Teotihuacan collapsed in the seventh or eighth centuries. When Aztecs later discovered the ruins, they gave the city its current name, which means "the birthplace of the gods." Mistaking the pyramids for tombs, they named its boulevard the Avenue of the Dead.

At about the time Rome was falling to the barbarians, Teotihuacan in nearby Mexico rivaled the great cities of the world in size and influence. A trip to this UNESCO World Heritage site provides an opportunity to see a collection of pyramids whose only real rivals are in Egypt.

A Monk and a Minaret

Ancient Minaret at Bosra, Syria

Bosra, an ancient city in southern Syria, contains the world's first minaret, a basalt structure inspired by a Christian bell tower. A monk from Bosra may also have helped form the religious views of Muhammad, the founder of Islam.

Egyptian records from 1400 B.C. refer to Bosra, which eventually came under the control of the Nabateans, the people of Petra. The Romans, who captured the city in the second century, made Bosra the capital of their Arabia province and built a still functioning 15,000 seat theater. Lying along the Roman road from Damascus to the Red Sea, Bosra later became a major Christian city, with a large sixth century cathedral attesting to its importance.

In 580 A.D., Muhammad, then about ten years old, reportedly stopped in Bosra with his uncle, a Meccan caravan driver. While there, Muhammad met with a monk named Bahira, who taught him about Christianity from the Nestorian (or perhaps Arian) perspective. Nestorian and Arian Christians rejected the belief that Jesus had been born divine and that Mary was the Mother of God, arguing that the notion of God producing offspring through a human mother had unmistakably pagan origins. As a result, they were considered heretics by orthodox Christians living further west.

According to Islamic tradition, Bahira told the young Muhammad he was destined to correct the mistaken views of orthodox Christianity about the nature of Jesus. The Quran, which Muhammad said came to him from an angel, says, speaking of God, "Far be it from His glory to have a son." So similar is this and comparable statements to the claims of Nestorians and Arians that some scholars believe the Quran builds on the tenets of non-orthodox Syrian Christianity Bahira taught Muhammad in Bosra, noting that Syrian Christians both then and now refer to God as "Allah."

Today, Bosra, a UNESCO World Heritage site, is a city of about 20,000 people, some living among the ancient ruins. Loud speakers atop the seventh century minaret still call the faithful to prayer. And most visitors leave unaware of the connections this city has to Islam, the fastest growing religion in the world.

Heaven on Earth

Church Floor at Taybet al Imam, Syria

In 1985, workers building a road in Taybet al Imam, a small town in northern Syria, uncovered a magnificent church floor buried beneath two feet of dirt. The floor, now protected under a permanent building, illustrates early Christian beliefs and may have provided the inspiration for Islamic images of Paradise.

The 6000 square-foot floor was once part of the Church of the Holy Martyrs, built in about 442 A.D. The floor still includes bases of columns that once supported the three-nave church. The entire floor is covered with colorful mosaic scenes, making it one of the largest continuous Byzantine mosaics ever found.

The scenes are not like those found in modern churches. No pictures show Jesus or Mary. None show saints or angels. In fact, the floor contains no representations of human or divine beings at all, reflecting the early Christian belief that God forbids the creation of graven images. Instead, the floor, likely built in the early sixth century, includes about 20 framed representations of important Christian buildings, including churches in Bethlehem and Jerusalem and the cross-shaped church honoring Simeon the Stylite.

The most theologically significant scenes illustrate the sixth century idea of Paradise. Many Christians then understood Paradise to be God's eventual recreation of the Garden of Eden on Earth, ushered in by the expected return of Jesus. So, deer drink from a steam overflowing with fish, wild animals run free and grapes and cool drinks are in abundance. Peacocks, whose bodies were once thought never to decay, drink from a golden chalice, symbolizing God's promise of immortality. Lions run together with prey among trees laden with fruit.

These images are remarkably similar to the Paradise described in the Quran, a fact not necessarily a coincidence. Muhammad is known to have visited Syrian churches during caravan trips with his uncle. As suggested by a floor panel showing two camels beside a caravan stop, the Church of the Holy Martyrs was along the caravan route north of Damascus. The Islamic images of Paradise may have their origins in a Syrian church.

Rock Center

Sacred Domes in Jerusalem

For some, the Dome of the Rock is just an image from a travel poster, identifying Jerusalem in the way the Eiffel Tower identifies Paris. But to billions of people, the famous golden dome, perched atop a blue porcelain base, is much more than a landmark—it shields a rock with enormous spiritual power.

The Dome of the Rock sits near the center of the Temple Mount, a 37-acre platform just across the Kidron Valley from the Mount of Olives, built by Herod the Great in 19 B.C. Most scholars agree that the Jewish Second Temple once stood on this platform. But when Islamic armies captured Jerusalem from the Byzantines in 634 A.D., the Second Temple was long gone, having been destroyed by the Romans in 70 A.D.

The new rulers of Jerusalem decided that the area surrounding an outcropping of rock on the flat surface of the Temple Mount would be the perfect spot for an imposing building announcing that Islam had arrived in the holy city toward which Muhammad and his followers had originally prayed. Reflecting Islam's nascent rivalry with Christianity, the Dome of the Rock, completed in 691 A.D., duplicated to within a few inches the dimensions of the blue-grey dome covering the tomb of Jesus on the nearby Church of the Holy Sepulchre, the holiest site in Christendom.

Most Muslims today associate the rock beneath the dome with a magical night ride they believe Muhammad made to Jerusalem in 621 A.D., from which he traveled to heaven and spoke with Abraham, Moses and Jesus. As a result, the Dome of the Rock and the Al-Aqsa Mosque of which it is a part are the third holiest sites of Sunni Islam, after Mecca and Medina. But many Jews and Christians believe the dome covers the rock on which Abraham had been willing to sacrifice his son, that King David later purchased for an altar to God and, most importantly, around which King Solomon, following God's instructions, built the First Temple. Ironically, Jerusalem's beautiful golden dome covers a rock at the very center of religious contention.

Honoring a Poem

Pancha Rathas Shrines near Mamallapuram, India

Monumental shrines carved in solid rock in southeast India pay homage to a poem that influences the lives of hundreds of millions of people every day. The shrines themselves, although never completed, have also had a lasting influence on the appearance of India.

Near the small town of Mamallapuram, about 40 miles south of Chennai along the Bay of Bengal, seventh century artisans sculpted five enormous shrines from a single outcropping of granite. The tallest of the intricately-carved shrines rises more than 35 feet from the sand and all include chambers for sheltering the images of one or more Hindu gods and goddesses. Inside one shrine, an adoring follower of Durga is famously shown cutting off her own head as a sacrifice to her goddess. In another, a statue merges the separate gods Shiva and Vishnu into a single, ecumenical image. Two lions and an elephant, carved from the same outcropping, stand guard.

The shrines are known collectively as Pancha Rathas (Five Chariots) because they reportedly suggest the wooden chariots used in ancient temple processions. Although originally intended to become temples, the shrines were never completed and therefore never consecrated. Long ago the residents of Mamallapuram decided to name the shrines in honor of the heroes of the *Mahabharata*, an epic poem completed in the fourth century A.D. that includes 1.8 million words and 200,000 verses, making it about eight times longer than the *Iliad* and the *Odyssey* combined. Included within the complex poem is the 700-verse *Bhagavad Gita*, a synthesis of moral and religious principles that is as important to Hindus as the Bible is to Christians. The *Mahabharata* recounts the story of five brothers of the Pandava family who battled their cousins for control of a legendary kingdom in northern India. Four of the Pancha Rathas are named for the Pandava brothers, two of whom were twins, and one is named for Draupadi, the wife they all shared.

The distinctive styles of the Pancha Rathas became models for later Hindu temples constructed throughout the Indian subcontinent. As a result, the shrines are now part of a UNESCO World Heritage site.

Wings and Rings

Eighteenth Century Bullring in Ronda, Spain

Ronda, a picturesque city in southern Spain, was once famous as the home of the first person to attempt to fly. Ronda is famous today as the home of the family that invented modern bullfighting.

Ronda, founded by Romans in the third century B.C., sits on a plateau split by a nearly 400-foot-deep canyon carved by the Guadalevin River. When Muslims from North Africa conquered southern Spain in 711 A.D., Ronda became an important center of Islamic culture and learning. Abbas Ibn Firnas, one of the great polymaths of Islam's Golden Age, was born in Ronda in 810 A.D. Among his inventions were corrective lenses, a method for cutting rock crystal, a water clock and a metronome to time his music. At age 65, he strapped feather-covered wings on his back and flew from a Cordoba mountain to a jarring, but otherwise safe, landing below.

Protected by its strategic location, Ronda was not captured by Christian forces of the *Reconquista* (Reconquest) until 1485. Its illustrious Islamic past was then forgotten as Muslims were driven from Spain. Modern Ronda visitors are not told about Abbas Ibn Firnas, but instead learn of Pedro Romero, a Ronda bullfighter who popularized his grandfather's novel idea of fighting bulls on foot using a gracefully maneuvered cape to conceal a sword for dispatching the bulls. Bullfighters previously killed from horseback, reflecting the hunting games from which bullfighting was apparently derived. Every September, the rich and famous come to Ronda for a week-long festival honoring Pedro Romero, who killed 5600 bulls, and Francisco de la Goya, who painted bullfighters and designed Romero's colorful outfits. Ronda's eighteenth century bullring, flanked by a statue of a bull poised to charge, now includes a museum of bullfighting. Nearby restaurants feature bull's tail, an acquired taste.

For his bullfighting exploits, Pedro Romero is honored by a statue in a Ronda park. For his frequent visits to Ronda's bullfights, Orson Welles is honored in a Ronda street name. For being the first man to fly, Abbas Ibn Firnas, forgotten in Ronda, is honored with his name on a crater on the moon.

A Body Divided

Basilica of St. Mark in Venice, Italy

More than 20 million visitors a year crowd colorful St. Mark's Square, where they mingle with jugglers, dancers, musicians, live statues and pigeons. Unknown to most visitors, for more than a thousand years Venetians have shared with Egypt their most prized possession—the bodily remains lying in the magnificent Basilica of St. Mark, often called The Church of Gold.

Venice, encompassing 188 islands strung together by about 400 bridges, is perhaps the most unusual city in the world, with canals serving as roads, boats serving as buses, and gondoliers serving as aphrodisiacs. From catching the water taxi docked at the airport to buying gelato from a street vendor to watching glass blowers create pieces of art in nearby Murano, nearly everything about the Venetian experience is unique.

Venice became a major maritime city-state during the middle ages, its power and wealth on display today in the palace of the doges who once ruled it. But in the early part of the ninth century, Venice lacked a suitable Christian relic commensurate with its growing power. So, in 832 A.D., Venetian merchants crossed the Mediterranean to Alexandria and stole the body claimed to be that of St. Mark, whom Egyptian Christians believe founded their church in 48 A.D. The remains were smuggled out of Egypt in a barrel of pork so the Muslim rulers of Alexandria would not inspect it. Or at least so goes the story reflected in thirteenth century mosaics on the front of the Basilica of St. Mark, built in the eleventh century on the site of an earlier church of the same name that had been constructed especially to hold the saint's body.

Egyptian (Coptic) Christians have long accepted the idea that the body of St. Mark now lies in Venice, but insist that the thieves somehow left his head behind, where it remains preserved in St. Mark's Coptic Orthodox Church in Alexandria. In 1968, Pope Paul VI, considered the successor of St. Peter by Roman Catholics, delivered to Pope Cyril VI, considered the successor of St. Mark by Coptic Christians, a bone fragment from Venice to rejoin the head in Alexandria.

Versailles of
the Middle Ages

Palace at Medina Azahara, near Cordoba, Spain

Medina Azahara (Shining City) near Cordoba, Spain, was the most dazzling city in the entire world during its very short life. Ironically, its premature demise allowed its architectural innovations to survive.

In 929 A.D., Abd-ar-Rahman III declared himself Caliph of Cordoba. Seeking to demonstrate that he was equal to his title, in 936 A.D. Rahman began building a magnificent new palace city on a 300-acre site in the foothills of the Sierra Morena a few miles west of Cordoba. The architects took advantage of the hillside by designing three terraces, the top reserved for the palace and the bottom for government workers. The middle terrace included a hall for receiving foreign ambassadors, covered with ivory and gold to impress the visitors. The hall also reportedly included a bowl of mercury the Caliph could jiggle to scatter reflected sunlight around the room.

When completed in about 976 A.D, Medina Azahara incorporated more than 4000 marble columns, some scavenged from as far away as Carthage. Most of the columns supported horseshoe arches, an architectural feature borrowed from the Visigoths but modified by alternating stones of different colors to call attention to the curved shape. Some of the arched columns separated courtyards from surrounding areas, a novel idea at the time. Formal Islamic gardens, watered by an aqueduct from the mountains, bordered the most important buildings. A modified Roman aqueduct served as a sewer. At the end of the tenth century, when Cordoba was the intellectual center of Europe, no city in the world could match the splendor of Medina Azahara.

In 1010, Berber forces battling for control of Cordoba destroyed Medina Azahara. The city was abandoned and many of the columns and arches were carried away and reused. Medina Azahara itself was soon buried and forgotten, but its architectural ideas, including the column-encircled courtyard and horseshoe arches, found their ways into buildings throughout southern Spain and eventually influenced the design of the Alhambra. Archaeologists who began excavating at Medina Azahara in 1911 have uncovered about 10 percent of the original city, including the palace and reception hall. The so-called "Versailles of the Middle Ages" is forgotten no more.

David's Empty Tomb

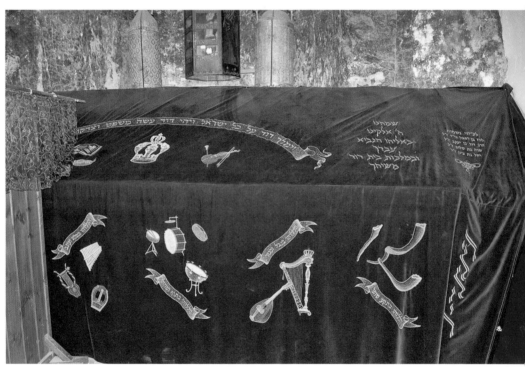

Traditional Sarcophagus of King David in Jerusalem

A building south of the Armenian section of Jerusalem's Old City is probably the only building on Earth deemed holy by Jews, Christians and Muslims. The building also shows how historical realities can become irrelevant in the face of religious traditions.

When the Crusaders captured Jerusalem in 1099 A.D., they discovered on Mt. Zion the ruins of a fourth century church that was once a synagogue. Muslim residents repeated stories from the tenth century that the synagogue was built over the tomb of Biblical King David. Christians said the church was associated with Jesus' last days on Earth. So the Crusaders erected the Church of St. Mary of Zion to honor both traditions. An empty stone box in a first floor room symbolized David's tomb and a larger space above was linked with the upper room where Jesus met with his disciples. When the Ottoman Turks gained control of Jerusalem, they added a minaret to the building and converted the upper room into a mosque honoring David, whom Muslims consider a prophet.

For about 800 years, Jewish residents of Jerusalem ignored claims associating the Crusader building with David because the Hebrew Scriptures say David is entombed in the City of David, hundreds of yards to the east. After the 1948 war, Jordan barred Jewish access to that and other important sites in Jerusalem, including the Western Wall. The tiny room with the stone box was one place having any claimed connection to Jewish history where Jews could gather to pray. So the box was covered with blue velvet richly embroidered with representations of musical instruments and Hebrew text proclaiming, "David the king of Israel lives forever." A small sign over the entrance proclaimed "King David's Tomb" in English, Hebrew and Arabic. Following Jewish tradition, only men now enter the "tomb" and women view the covered box through an opening in the wall.

Jews pray in King David's Tomb on the first floor, Christians pray in the upper room and Muslims pray on the roof. No one cares if David is really in his tomb.

Time Machine
to a Golden Age

Tannery in Fes el Bali, Morocco

At a time when much of Europe was still intellectually asleep, Fes el Bali (Old Fes) was the "Athens of Africa." Today this walled city within Fes, Morocco, is the world's largest automobile free urban area, with 9000 twisting streets so narrow in places that loaded donkeys cannot easily pass.

Idris I, the grandson of Muhammad, founded the city of Fes el Bali in 789 A.D. as the capital of his new Islamic Empire. The University of Al-Karaouine, now the world's oldest university, was established in the city in 859 A.D. By the twelfth century, Fes el Bali had become an international center of Islamic learning and culture. Its population of 200,000 made it the largest city in the world. When Maimonides, the great Jewish philosopher and physician, left Cordoba, Spain, in about 1160 because of growing tension between Jews and Muslims, he settled in Fes el Bali to continue his studies.

For Fes el Bali's 150,000 current residents, life is not much different than it was hundreds of years ago, although electricity makes some tasks easier. Merchants in small shops still sell everything from fresh camel and goat meat on hooks to fruit and fish stacked high on tables to pottery and clothing made by hand. Two hundred mosques still call residents to prayer. One popular shop sells rugs woven by Berbers in the nearby Atlas Mountains and another sells high-end antiques in a fourteenth century mansion.

Tanneries producing leather using processes unchanged since the twelfth century have become symbols of Fes el Bali. Employees hand visitors mint sprigs to hold under their noses as they observe huge vats where hides, gathered daily from local slaughter houses, are tanned and colored. The mint can't overcome the stench of the tanning agent, made from pigeon droppings and said to be the secret to the suppleness of the brightly colored leather goods sold in tannery shops.

Major construction projects are changing the face of Morocco. Fes el Bali, a UNESCO World Heritage site, is protected against the rush of the twenty first century and provides the closest approximation we have to a time machine to Morocco's golden age.

Death of a Temple

Sahasra Baahu Temple Complex, near Udaipur, India

Near the city of Udaipur in northwest India is a Hindu temple complex called Sahasra Baahu, built more than 1000 years ago. The intricate stone carvings both inside and out reflect countless hours of tedious effort. But the complex and the extraordinary human effort it represents now lie abandoned, not because no worshippers are nearby but because the temple has literally lost its soul.

For most Hindus, the ultimate reality of the universe is Brahman, a transcendent and unknowable power behind and beyond all existence. The many images of Hindu gods found throughout India are embraceable manifestations of the divine, worshipped by people incapable of wrapping their minds around the incomprehensible nature of Brahman. Somewhat like Christians with a guardian angel, many Hindus consider themselves monotheists despite praying to specific manifestations of the ultimate reality for help and guidance.

To worship their chosen manifestations of Brahman, Hindus have long built temples having the essential characteristics of temples everywhere. At the center is the Holy of Holies, where the statutory image resides. Above the Holy of Holies, a pyramid-shaped tower points toward the heavens. On the walls are carvings having religious significance. Surprising to many Christians, for whom God and sexual pleasure don't usually mix, the walls of Hindu temples often contain explicit sex scenes, not always procreative. Hindus find the divine in all human activity and nothing is shameful about the desire for pleasure. The wildly colorful exteriors of many Hindu temples demonstrate this same idea.

When Sahasra Baahu was completed in the tenth or eleventh century, a stone image of the god Vishnu was placed in the Holy of Holies. A priest then called the power of Brahman into the statue. Once so consecrated, the temple became alive and worshippers could experience the divine within it.

Today, no image resides in Sahasra Baahu's Holy of Holies. Probably hundreds of years ago the statue was damaged, likely by persons opposing Hindu beliefs. As a result, the temple died, never to live again. With the spirit of the eternal Brahman missing, the magnificent stone carvings have no more spiritual significance than a pile of rocks.

The Glitz and the Ghastly

The Tower of London

The Tower of London, a UNESCO World Heritage site, is one of England's most popular destinations. Well-rehearsed Beefeaters explain its history with ghoulish delight and the crown jewels dazzle visitors riding past them on a people mover. But the glib and the glitz mingle with the ghastly.

At the heart of the 18-acre Tower complex is a castle erected in 1078 by William the Conqueror after he crossed the English Channel and defeated Anglo-Saxon King Harold. A series of buildings were added later in two concentric circles around the original castle. Although used for many purposes, the Tower of London has served as a prison almost from the beginning and its stone towers have been the scenes of crimes and intrigue.

The so-called "Bloody Tower" memorializes two young princes murdered there by their uncle, the future King Richard III. The Wakefield Tower, where King Henry VI was murdered as he prayed, displays a collection of instruments of torture, used to extract "confessions" from those whose religious beliefs didn't match those of the monarch. The most frequently used instrument was the Duke of Exeter's Daughter, named after the Constable of the Tower who introduced it. Ropes wound around oppositely rotating drums stretched the victim on a rack, inducing pain so severe that a confession was almost inevitable.

Although known for its beheadings, the Tower of London itself was the scene of only a few executions. Condemned prisoners not deserving the privacy of a Tower execution were killed on nearby Tower Hill, their newly severed heads held high for the cheering crowds. As told by the Beefeaters, Tower executioners were notoriously inept, one taking eleven whacks of his axe before finishing off the Countess of Salisbury. Another, a butcher by trade, completed his job with a knife. Anne Boleyn, the wife of Henry VIII, was afforded the courtesy of a French swordsman, who dispatched her on the Tower green with one stroke.

A trip to London isn't complete without a visit to the Tower. But expect not only to be entertained, but to be reminded of how cruel human beings can be to each other, often in the name of religion.

Origins of an Icon

Eleventh Century Fresco of St. George in Cappadocia, Turkey

The Cappadocia region of central Turkey, home to Christian communities since the second century, includes dozens of churches carved inside the area's unique volcanic rock formations. An eleventh century fresco in one church honored St. George, a favorite son, and originated an iconic image seen in churches around the world.

St. George was apparently born in about 275 A.D. in Lydda, Palestine, where his Cappadocian father had met his mother while serving in the Roman army. George, raised a Christian, became an officer in the military guard of Emperor Diocletian. In 303 A.D. Diocletian ordered his officers to repudiate Christianity or face death. When George refused to renounce his beliefs, he was tortured and then beheaded. Emperor Constantine reportedly ordered a church built in Lydda to honor George, who became a saint in 494 A.D. Over time, St. George became associated with a medieval legend in which a maiden-devouring dragon terrorized a pagan village. As the story went, George slew the dragon and the grateful villagers all converted to Christianity.

In the eleventh century, numerous Byzantine churches were built within the soft, cone-shaped rocks of Cappadocia. Frescoes, still colorful because of the absence of direct sunlight, decorated many of them. One fresco on a curved wall in the so-called "Snake Church" (Yılanlı Kilise) honors St. George, whose father was raised nearby. The fresco portrays a haloed and armored George, sitting astride a festooned white horse and gouging a snakelike dragon with his lance. St. George is accompanied in the fresco, perhaps the earliest illustration of the legend, by St. Theodore of Amasea, a less well-known Christian martyr also associated with dragon slaying. Crusaders passing through Cappadocia took the story of St. George and the dragon back to Europe, with the dragon often assumed to represent Satan.

The image in Cappadocia's Snake Church of a battle-bedecked St. George, atop a white horse and killing a dragon with a lance, inspired countless imitations and became a familiar icon in Eastern Orthodox and Roman Catholic churches. The Göreme Open Air Museum, which includes the Snake Church, became a UNESCO World Heritage site in 1984.

Castles and Knights

Crac des Chevaliers, near Homs, Syria

Syria's Crac des Chevaliers is the best preserved Crusader castle in the world. Its fortifications foiled one of the most capable military leaders in history and have survived the current war in Syria.

Crac des Chevaliers is located atop a volcanic mound along a pass between the port city of Tripoli, Lebanon, and Homs, Syria. The first fortress on the site was built by the Kurds in about 1031 to protect Homs from a sea-borne attack. That fortress was captured in 1110 during the First Crusade and then anchored Tripoli County, a Crusader State. In about 1142, the Count of Tripoli donated the castle to the Knights Hospitaller, a Christian order that arose to assist pilgrims in the Holy Land and evolved into a fighting force to retain the lands taken during the Crusades.

The Hospitallers converted the original Kurdish fortress into the most elaborate of their many castles in the Middle East, calling it Crac de l'Ospital. The central living and administrative buildings, including a large chapel, were separated from a massive outer wall by a wide moat. Areas for storing grain, olive oil and water were designed to enable a garrison of 2000 soldiers and their horses to withstand a five-year siege. Visiting Crusaders returned to Europe with novel ideas for their own castles.

By 1187, Saladin, the great Muslim ruler, had retaken most of the lands occupied by the Crusaders, including Jerusalem. He then turned his attention to recapturing the territory controlled by the Knights Hospitaller from their base at Crac des Chevaliers. After viewing what he considered the castle's impregnable fortifications, Saladin did not even attempt an attack. The castle finally fell to Baybars, a Mamluk Sultan, in 1271 after a siege that reportedly ended with a forged directive telling the Hospitallers to surrender. The conquerors turned the castle's chapel into a mosque.

Crac des Chevaliers, near the contested city of Homs, has been shelled by both sides in Syria's civil war. The castle, a UNESCO World Heritage site, has sustained damage but remains largely intact, a tribute to the Knights who designed and built it.

Muslims Hold the Key

Church of the Holy Sepulchre in Jerusalem

For many Christians, Jerusalem's Church of the Holy Sepulchre, said to encompass both the site of Jesus' crucifixion and his tomb, is the holiest place on Earth. Ironically, maintaining peace in this sprawling basilica requires that Muslims hold onto its only key.

In 326 A.D., Emperor Constantine ordered a church built on the site of a Roman temple after his mother Helena claimed to have learned during a visit to Jerusalem that the temple covered Jesus' tomb. During construction, Helena is said to have discovered the "true cross" on which Jesus was crucified and a chapel was built on the site of that discovery. Different Christian groups later built additional chapels near the original church.

During the Crusades, all the structures now constituting the Church of the Holy Sepulchre were consolidated under a single roof and a single entrance. Six Christian groups ended up controlling parts of the same building. Because of their different beliefs and traditions, these groups have long squabbled over everything from the theological to the territorial. They have not even been able to agree on which of them should possess the ancient key to the only entrance. As a result, since 1187 the key to the Church of the Holy Sepulchre has been held by two local Muslim families, one of which opens the church while the other closes it.

In 1853, in an effort to eliminate ongoing disputes, a formal agreement was reached to maintain the status quo. It has not worked. In 2002, a Coptic monk moved a chair about eight inches from its traditional location. The ensuing melee sent 11 people to the hospital. In 2004, another fight broke out after a traditionally closed door was left open.

Before 1853, someone placed a small wooden ladder below a second story window to the right of the entrance. With no agreement on a new location, the ladder cannot be moved. In 1964, Pope Paul VI decreed that this so-called "immovable ladder" should stay put until the Great Schism of 1054 that divides the Roman Catholic and Eastern Orthodox churches has been overcome. The world waits.

Images in Istanbul

Anastasis *Fresco in Chora Church in Istanbul, Turkey*

After touring Hagia Sophia, many visitors assume they have seen the best Byzantine art in Istanbul. They have not. What may be the most impressive collection of medieval mosaics and frescoes in the world can now be seen because they were once considered blasphemous.

The Church of Christ the Savior in Chora in western Istanbul derives its name from a fourth century monastery in the same location, which was outside the walls of Constantinople and therefore in *chora*, Greek for "the countryside." Byzantine Emperor Justinian I built a church on the site in the sixth century, apparently because it was near his summer palace. After additions and improvements, the building became associated with the Orthodox Church after its split from the Roman Catholic Church in the Great Schism of 1054. The church attained most of its current configuration in about 1081.

In 1204, Catholic participants in the Fourth Crusade sacked Constantinople and significantly damaged the church. After Orthodox forces recaptured Constantinople in 1261, Theodore Metochites, a wealthy statesman and patron of the arts, restored the church and covered its interior with dozens of colorful mosaics and frescoes depicting the life and death of Jesus, Biblical stories and characters and scenes important to the church. The renderings are more intricate than typical art of the period. One colorful mosaic shows Metochites handing the church to Jesus. A complex gold-leaf mosaic depicts the bodily assumption of Mary into heaven. The most famous of the frescoes, labeled *Anastasis* (resurrection), is on a dome near the burial chapel. Frequently emulated, it shows the returned Jesus giving a hand to Adam and Eve as they arise bodily from their graves, with other Biblical figures watching nearby.

In 1453, when the Ottoman Turks conquered Constantinople and renamed it Istanbul, they turned the Chora Church into a mosque, complete with a minaret. Because Islam forbids graven images, they covered the mosaics and frescoes with plaster, inadvertently preserving them. Beginning in 1948, the Turkish government uncovered and restored the images and reopened the church in 1958 as a museum. Many visitors to Istanbul overlook the splendors of the Chora Church. Don't be among them.

Cry for Me!

Citadel of Aleppo, Syria, in November 2010

Aleppo, Syria, is the oldest continuously inhabited city in the world. Until the Syrian civil war, it was also one of the most inclusive cities in the Middle East. That fighting is gradually destroying the city, the ancient center of which is a UNESCO World Heritage site.

At the heart of Aleppo is a medieval citadel atop a strategic hill inhabited for at least 5000 years. A local legend claims Abraham raised goats on the hill and provided milk for travelers on the caravan route between the Mediterranean and Mesopotamia. From the earliest times, the hill included both fortresses and shrines to the favorite gods of the rulers of the day, from the Amorite Hadad to the Roman Zeus. Byzantine Christians built churches in the citadel, which were converted to mosques, one named for Abraham, when Muslims conquered Aleppo in 636 A.D. Aleppo's citadel later served as a prison for captured Crusaders. The citadel was expanded to its current configuration under Az-Zahir Ghazi, the son of Saladin who ruled Aleppo in the thirteenth century. Ghazi converted the citadel into an opulent palace, complete with private baths. Later rulers enhanced city walls encompassing the citadel, the main mosque and a covered souk (market) approximately eight miles long.

After the Ottomans gained control of Aleppo, the city became an important center of international trade. Major European countries opened consulates in Aleppo, which took on a distinctly western feel while maintaining its famous souk, ancient gates and other reminders of its eastern heritage. Shakespeare referred to Aleppo in both *Macbeth* and *Othello*. Christians, especially from Armenia, moved to Aleppo, creating what was the largest concentration of Christians in Syria. The active Forty Martyrs Cathedral, located in the Christian quarter, was built in 1491.

Aleppo has seen some of the fiercest fighting of the Syrian Civil War, with all sides accusing the others of atrocities and indiscriminate damage to important historical sites, including the citadel and the souk. The minaret of Aleppo's main mosque, erected in 1090, was destroyed by tank fire. Unfortunately, the city named the Islamic Capital of Culture for 2006 will never be the same.

The Magic Pillar

Qutb Minar Complex in Delhi, India

The Qutb Minar complex in Delhi, a UNESCO World Heritage site, is one of India's top attractions. Visitors marvel at the tallest all-brick tower in the world, completed almost 650 years ago, and at an unpainted iron pillar that has not rusted for almost 1700 years.

The Qutb Minar complex is named for Qutb al-Din Aybak, a slave turned general from Afghanistan who conquered northern India in 1192, destroying at least 27 Hindu and Jain temples in the process. In 1206, Qutb al-Din Aybak declared himself Sultan of Delhi and began building a brick victory tower incorporating rubble from the demolished temples. When he fell from his polo horse and died in 1210, his successors continued his work. The fluted sandstone tower, adorned with statements from the Quran, was topped off in 1368 at a height of 238 feet, about 50 feet higher than the contemporaneously constructed tower in Pisa, Italy. With 379 internal steps and five circular balconies, Qutb Minar has become a symbol of Delhi.

 As the Muslim conquerors under Qutb al-Din Aybak demolished the temples at the site on which they later built Qutb Minar, they intentionally spared a 22-foot-tall iron pillar erected in the fourth century to honor Vishnu, a Hindu god. They spared the 16.4-inch diameter pillar because of its apparently magical ability to resist rust, a property scientists now attribute to phosphorus added by Hindu metallurgists. So unusual is a rust-free iron pillar that people still believe their wishes will be granted if they can encircle the pillar with their arms stretched behind their backs. A fence now protects the pillar from pilgrims seeking to improve their luck.

The beauty and continued existence of Qutb Minar are tributes to its Muslim designers. The nearby iron pillar reflects the genius of Hindu metallurgists. A visit to the Qutb Minar complex therefore reminds us that many cultures have produced works of lasting importance. A visit also provides an opportunity to bemoan the need members of religious traditions unfortunately still have to try to show the superiority of their faiths by destroying the holy places of those with different beliefs.

Built for a Crown

Second Floor of Sainte Chapelle in Paris, France

After visitors to Paris have seen the Eiffel Tower, they usually head to Île de la Cité, an island in the Seine, to see Notre Dame, one of the largest and most famous churches in the world. They usually don't even notice nearby Sainte Chapelle, a Holy Chapel that many consider a more beautiful example of medieval church architecture.

The two-story Sainte Chapelle was constructed between 1239 and 1248 by French King Louis IX adjacent his palace on Île de la Cité. The ground floor chapel, built for the palace staff, is impressive in its own right. But it is the chapel on the second floor, originally accessible directly from the palace, which is the masterpiece. This chapel for the king and his court, now reached by a steep stairway from the first floor, includes sidewalls more than 50 feet high consisting largely of thousands of tiny pieces of stained glass illuminating stories from the Bible. Especially on sunny days, the vaulted ceiling seems to float ethereally above the walls.

King Louis ordered the building of Sainte Chapelle as an elaborate reliquary for his most prized possession – a crown of thorns claimed to be the one placed on Jesus' head before he was crucified 1200 years before. Louis acquired this relic in 1238 from its cash-strapped owner, Emperor Baldwin II of Constantinople, who had pawned it to the Venetians to secure a debt of 13,134 gold pieces. For his lifelong support of the church, including acquiring the crown of thorns, building Sainte Chapelle and serving in the Seventh and Eighth Crusades, which led to his death in 1270, Louis was declared a saint in 1297, the only French king so honored.

If you get a chance to visit Paris, after exploring Notre Dame stop by St. Louis' magnificent chapel just a few blocks away. Since his palace in the Seine is now the French Palace of Justice, entering Sainte Chapelle requires first going through government security. But seeing such an inspiring achievement of human creativity is well worth the minimal effort and you will be glad you stopped.

Piazzas, Popes
and Bleeding Bread

Thirteenth Century Clock Tower in Orvieto, Italy

The small Italian city of Orvieto (Old City) was founded by the Etruscans atop a butte formed from soft volcanic rock. The sides of the butte are so steep that a funicular now takes visitors from the train station and parking lots to the city 700 feet above. Because of its secure location, lying along the road between Florence and Rome, medieval Popes often lived in Orvieto and the city reflects that history.

The most visible evidence of papal influence is Orvieto's cathedral, located on the main square and unexpectedly large for a city of only 10,000. The cathedral is one of the most colorful in Europe, with horizontal stone striping both inside and out and a façade lavishly covered with paintings and mosaics. Dedicated to the Assumption of the Virgin, builders started construction of the cathedral in 1290 and continued for hundreds of years. One chapel in the cathedral features frescoes of the Apocalypse by Luca Signorelli, the inspiration for Michelangelo's famous *Last Judgment* in the Sistine Chapel. Another chapel houses a communion cloth stained when the host began bleeding, convincing a skeptical priest in the nearby town of Bolsena that the consecrated bread really did become the body of Jesus. Persistent claims that the entire cathedral was built to celebrate this "miracle of Bolsena" are not true and skeptics assert the stains came from bread mold.

In 1527, Pope Clement VII escaped to Orvieto during the sack of Rome by mutinous forces once loyal to Emperor Charles V. Fearing a siege, the Pope ordered construction of the 175-foot-deep St. Patrick's Well, named for an Irish legend that deep wells provide access to Purgatory. The central shaft is surrounded by two helixes allowing donkeys (and modern visitors) to pass each other as they travel up and down fetching water.

Pleasant cafes in the car-free piazzas of Orvieto feature the wines for which the city is famous. Shops feature ceramics, made in Orvieto since the days of the Etruscans. An afternoon in Orvieto, a short train ride from Rome, is an ideal respite from the bustle of the Eternal City.

The Cathedral
in the Mosque

Inside the Mezquita of Cordoba, Spain

Young Christian girls in Spain dream of marrying in the Mezquita, the Great Mosque of Cordoba. At the same time, Muslims are barred from praying in the building that illustrates the best of early Islamic architecture and manifests Spain's turbulent religious history.

During the early first millennium A.D., the Mezquita's current location was the site of a temple to Janus, the Roman god of beginnings. In the sixth century, Cordoba was captured by the Visigoths, Germanic Christians deemed heretics by the established church because they refused to accept the divinity of Jesus. After their leader converted to orthodox Christianity in 589 A.D., the Visigoths razed the temple and built a church, whose mosaic floor can be seen through a cut-out in the floor of the Mezquita.

Muslims from North Africa conquered Cordoba in 711 A.D. and used part of the Visigoth church as their mosque. Later in the eighth century, Abd al-Rahman I, an exile from Syria, established an Islamic dynasty centered in Cordoba and reportedly purchased the site of the Visigoth church for a mosque modeled on the Great Mosque of Damascus. The mosque was expanded by al-Rahman I's successors until it covered almost six acres. A flat wooden roof, capable of shading 20,000 worshippers, was supported by 856 Roman columns from earlier buildings, their heights extended by novel double brick and stone arches suggesting palm trees.

In 1236 Christians reconquered Cordoba, at the time one of the most important cities in the world. Instead of demolishing the Great Mosque, as they had other Spanish mosques, church leaders removed a large section of the roof and the columns supporting it and erected an ornate cathedral in the middle of the mosque. The cathedral, incorporating gothic, baroque and renaissance themes, remains surrounded by the original columns.

When Holy Roman Emperor Charles V observed the mutilation of the mosque by the embedded church, he reportedly expressed regret at having authorized the construction. That decision nonetheless preserved most of the Mezquita, now a UNESCO World Heritage site and Spain's second most visited location.

The Bells of St. Mary's

Memorial Chapel of St. Mary's Church in Lübeck, Germany

Lübeck, in the northern German state of Schleswig-Holstein, was one of the most important cities in Europe during the late Middle Ages. Today, the city features magnificent medieval architecture and a poignant message from World War II.

Henry the Lion, a powerful German prince, founded Lübeck in 1159 on an island surrounded by rivers linking the German interior to the Baltic Sea. By the thirteenth century, Lübeck, with a population of 25,000, had grown rich trading such items as fish, wood and salt. Controlled by local merchants, the town put its wealth into imposing buildings, from glazed-brick city gates and a monumental town hall, to five churches boasting a total of seven spires. Lübeck's grandest architectural achievement was twin-towered St. Mary's Church, erected adjacent the town hall from 1250 to 1350. Lacking sandstone, builders executed in brick the Gothic style becoming popular further south, creating what remains, at 126 feet, the world's tallest brick vault. The design of St. Mary's inspired dozens of imitators around the Baltic. By the fifteenth century, Lübeck was the Queen City of the Hanseatic League, an alliance of northern European market towns.

In the early morning hours of March 29, 1942, Palm Sunday, 234 Royal Air Force bombers attacked Lübeck in the first substantial air raid on a German city. Buildings were set afire by a combination of blockbuster bombs and incendiary devices. About 20 percent of the town was destroyed and 301 residents were killed in the resulting firestorm. Three of Lübeck's ancient churches were severely damaged. Bells hanging in the 410-foot-high towers of St. Mary's reportedly rang out as they fell into the blazing church.

Visitors to Lübeck, a UNESCO World Heritage site, can walk up a curving cobblestone street from the single remaining town gate to the old town center, passing gabled townhouses of thirteenth century merchants. The most significant medieval structures have been meticulously restored, with one notable exception. The shattered bells of St. Mary's lie in a small corner chapel, just as they alighted, a reminder that war's devastation respects neither religion nor history.

An Image of Paradise

Courtyard of the Maidens in Real Alcázar in Seville, Spain

The Real Alcázar (Royal Palace) in Seville, Spain, is the oldest European palace still being used. Important parts of what is now a UNESCO World Heritage site were built by a fourteenth-century Christian king who admired Islamic architecture and became known for his brutal rejection of anti-Semitism.

When Christian forces of the *Reconquista* recaptured Seville in 1248, they took as their palace an Islamic fortress along the Guadalquivir River. In 1364, Peter I, King of Castile and León, began building a new palace on the site. Peter called upon the Muslim architects and builders who had recently created the palace at the Alhambra in Granada, then still under Islamic control. The design style used in Peter's palace, incorporating richly carved walls, pointed arches and other traditional Islamic details, came to be known as *mudéjar* and was popular throughout southern Spain. Writings on palace walls praised both God and Allah.

The best-known quarter of Peter's palace is the Courtyard of the Maidens. Its name reportedly suggested a false rumor, fueling the *Reconquista*, that Muslim rulers of Iberia demanded 100 virgins each year from the Christian cities under their control. A narrow reflecting pool in the center of the courtyard was flanked by sunken gardens, evoking Islamic images of the gardens of Paradise. The same theme was later used in the reflecting pool of the Taj Mahal. Scalloped arches supported on columns surrounded the open courtyard, another defining characteristic of mudéjar style.

Peter I's rivals called him Peter the Cruel for executing leaders of an anti-Jewish riot. He was beheaded in 1369 by his half-brother Henry, who derided him as King of the Jews for opposing persecution of Spanish Jews.

King Peter's successors added buildings and gardens to the Real Alcázar. The second floor of Peter's palace is used by the Spanish royal family when in Seville. The Courtyard of the Maidens, its reflecting pool covered, masquerades as the twelfth century palace of the King of Jerusalem in the movie *The Kingdom of Heaven*. And history now regards Peter I as Peter the Just for repudiating, albeit cruelly, religious bigotry.

Treasures of
the Palace

Topkapı Palace in Istanbul, Turkey

The Topkapı Palace is the most visited spot in Istanbul. One of the reasons for this popularity is its claim to house an unrivaled collection of ancient religious treasures important to Jews, Christians and Muslims.

In 1453, Muslim forces under 21-year-old Sultan Mehmed II conquered Constantinople, the last bastion of the Byzantine Empire. Mehmed renamed the city Istanbul and proclaimed it the capital of his Ottoman Empire. For his new palace he selected a 175-acre site on a hill overlooking the Bosporus that separates Europe from Asia. When completed, what became known as the Topkapı Palace comprised dozens of buildings scattered among four large courtyards, reportedly suggesting earlier Ottoman tent encampments. At its peak, the palace accommodated 4000 people, including hundreds of concubines eager to catch the sultan's eye and bear his son. An enormous kitchen, with 10 domes, 20 chimneys and a staff of 800, provided thousands of meals every day. A handsome library stored 3500 important manuscripts, including an early copy of the Quran. The Tower of Justice, visible from the Bosporus, symbolized the reputed fairness of the sultan, whose justice included public beheadings in the first courtyard near the Byzantine church of Hagia Irene.

After the Ottoman Empire collapsed in 1923, the palace was converted to a museum. The ticket booth is near an ornate fountain where the executioner reportedly washed his sword after exacting the sultan's justice. The former treasury building displays the 86-carat Spoonmaker's Diamond, the world's fourth largest diamond. What were once private rooms of the sultans now display religious relics collected from around the empire. For Muslims, the cloak, sword, banner and beard hairs of Muhammad are the most revered. Visitors who check their skepticism at the gate can also view the cooking pot of Abraham, the staff of Moses, the coat of Joseph, the sword of David and the right hand of John the Baptist.

In 2013, the Topkapı Palace surpassed Hagia Sophia as the most popular destination in Istanbul, with the faithful often lined up to see the religious items. A visit to the harem, once supervised by the sultan's mother, requires a separate ticket.

A Temple from a Dream

Jain Temple at Ranakpur, India

In the tiny village of Ranakpur, near Udaipur in western India, is the best known and most elaborate of the temples of Jainism, a religion founded in India at about the same time as Buddhism. Construction of this spectacular 48,000 square-foot temple, made entirely of light marble, began in 1439 A.D. When completed 19 years later, the temple included 1444 exquisitely carved columns, no two of them alike. The temple's 29 halls and 80 domes are also decorated with labyrinthine carvings, many of people and animals. Remarkable as these carvings are, even more remarkable are the beliefs of the people who still worship in this temple.

The fundamental beliefs of Jainism are apparent even before entering the temple, when visitors must first remove anything made of leather. Jains believe that every living thing has a soul and see it as their primary duty to honor anything that is or was alive. Aggressively non-violent, Jains often wear masks over their noses and mouths to avoid accidentally swallowing insects. All Jains are vegetarians and many won't eat anything that came from tilling the soil because farming leads to the death of small animals. Many eat only nuts and fruit that have already fallen to avoid hurting the trees and refuse to be carpenters who hurt the wood they work.

Jains are very respectful of other religious beliefs, believing that all religions, including their own, reflect only an imperfect understanding of ultimate reality. The design of the Ranakpur temple witnesses this conviction. Four doors, one on each side of the temple, all lead to the center, where the four-faced statue of Adinatha, the revered traditional founder of Jainism, is enshrined. No matter which path is taken, the entrant inevitably encounters an image of the divine.

The almost surreal design of the Ranakpur temple is said to have been inspired by a dream divinely sent to its architect. The temple and the beliefs of those who worship in it can inspire another type of dream—a dream of a world in which everyone's reverence for life and respect for the beliefs of others are at least a little more like those of the Jains.

A Legendary Cape

Cape of Good Hope from Cape Point, South Africa

Cape Point, a UNESCO World Heritage site situated 30 miles south of Cape Town, South Africa, offers an extraordinary view of the famous Cape of Good Hope, which is neither the southernmost point of Africa nor the point where oceans meet. It is, however, the home of a macabre legend.

In 1487, Portuguese explorer Bartholomew Diaz and his crew sailed south from Lisbon along the western coast of Africa, hoping to find a sea route to India. Diaz managed to sail east after reaching the southern coast of Africa, but his frightened sailors refused to continue. On the return trip, Diaz encountered a rocky headland jutting into the ocean that he named The Cape of Storms because of violent weather in the area. His patron, King John II, renamed the point the Cape of Good Hope because it proved sailing to India was feasible.

The king's optimism was justified. In 1498, Vasco de Gama "rounded the Cape of Good Hope" and continued until he reached India. The notion of "rounding the Cape" has long suggested that the Cape of Good Hope is at the southern tip of Africa. It is not. To the east, little-known Cape Agulhas extends further south. Cape Agulhas is also where the warm currents of the Indian Ocean bump up against the cooler currents of the South Atlantic, creating turbulent weather. Cape Point tourists, having never heard of Cape Agulhas, buy t-shirts incorrectly saying they have seen "where two oceans meet."

To reach the hilltop offering the best view of the Cape of Good Hope, visitors to Cape Point ride The Flying Dutchman, a funicular named for a legendary Dutch ship reportedly lost off the Cape of Good Hope during a storm. According to a seventeenth century tale, the ship and its ghostly crew are destined to sail the oceans forever, foretelling doom to anyone catching sight of the glowing ship. After seeing the Cape of Good Hope, the adventuresome can look for 250 species of birds and several troops of baboons. They can also try to avoid spotting the Flying Dutchman.

At the Center of 1492

The Alhambra's Hall of Ambassadors in Granada, Spain

During 1492, the Alhambra in Grenada, Spain, was at the center of events that literally changed the direction of human history. Today the Alhambra is the finest example of Islamic architecture in Europe.

Grenada was founded in the eleventh century by successors of Muslims who had captured most of what is now Spain from the Visigoths in 711 A.D. By 1248 A.D., Christian forces had recaptured all major Spanish cities except Granada. Grenada, whose Muslim rulers welcomed its Jewish residents, became one of the most important cities in Europe. In the fourteenth century, Grenada's Nasrid rulers completed the Alhambra on a hill overlooking the city as a combined fortress and palace. The main courtyard surrounded a circle of twelve marble lions, representing the twelve tribes of Israel, carved by Jewish craftsmen. The palace included an imposing Hall of Ambassadors, where the Sultan of Granada received visitors.

On January 2, 1492, the Sultan surrendered the Alhambra to the superior forces of Ferdinand II and Isabella I, the Catholic Kings whose marriage had united two Spanish kingdoms. Isabella immediately occupied the chair in the Hall of Ambassadors, reportedly receiving Christopher Columbus. Columbus, who had seen Granada fall, pitched anew his plan to sail west and convert the Muslims of India to Christianity.

The Alhambra Decree, issued by Ferdinand and Isabella on March 31, 1492, ordered all Jews to leave Spain within four months unless they converted to Christianity. On April 17, Ferdinand and Isabella commissioned Columbus to sail to India and he left Granada on May 12. By July 31, up to 800,000 Jewish residents had fled Spain to avoid execution without trial. On October 12, 1492, Columbus, who may have been secretly Jewish, encountered the lands of the "New World" he insisted to his death were part of India.

In April 1992, five hundred years after the Alhambra Decree, Spanish King Juan Carlos, wearing a yarmulke, welcomed descendants of the expelled Sephardic (Spanish) Jews back to Spain, where they can now become citizens. The Alhambra, a UNESCO World Heritage site, is witness to the best and the worst of Spanish history.

Built for Love

Adalaj Stepwell, near Ahmedabad, India

Visitors to India are accustomed to looking up for the achievements of Indian architects. But uniquely Indian structures called stepwells lie below the surface and are as fascinating as tombs and temples. One of the most famous also comes with a classic Indian love story.

Weather on the Indian subcontinent is characterized by periods of intense rain followed by long periods of drought. Because the soil is usually not suitable for reservoirs, Indians in the fifth century began building structures with hollow stone shafts extending up to 50 feet below the surface. Steps led from the surface to the shaft's bottom, with periodic landings allowing people to congregate on various levels. When the rains came, the structure filled with water and people drew water and bathed near the top. As water was consumed, people descended the steps until they reached the water level. Because Hindus believe waters create a boundary between Earth and heaven, representations of gods and other religious symbols on the landings enabled people to engage in underground religious ceremonies surrounded by water.

The Adalaj stepwell near Ahmedabad, Gujarat, is one of the most famous, both for its design and the story of its origins. According to Sanskrit writings on a marble slab near the bottom, the Adalaj stepwell was begun by a Hindu king named Veer Singh who was killed in battle by a Muslim leader named Mohammed Begda. Begda took over the kingdom and pined for the king's widow, the beautiful Roopba. Roopba promised Begda she would marry him but only if he first completed her husband's stepwell. Begda completed the project in 1499, with an octagonal shaft lavishly covered with both Hindu and Islamic images extending five stories below the surface. With Roopba's goal of honoring her husband accomplished, she then jumped to her death in the shaft.

India's stepwells were abandoned when the English declared them unsanitary, but many have been restored. The next time you get to India, look down after you have seen the Taj Mahal and the famous temples. Not all stepwells come with a legendary story, but all reflect the ingenuity of Indian architects.

What Remains of Columbus?

Christopher Columbus's Tomb in Seville, Spain

Seville, a beautiful city in southern Spain, is famous for more than its barber. Seville's archive of original writings documenting the story of fifteenth and sixteenth century Spanish explorers is a UNESCO World Heritage site. Seville also holds at least part of what was once Christopher Columbus.

By the fifteenth century, Seville had become one of the most prosperous cities in Europe, profiting enormously from trade passing through its inland port. The cathedral was begun in 1401 to show Seville's wealth to the entire Christian world. When completed more than 100 years later, the cathedral covered more than 100,000 square feet and is the second largest cathedral in Europe.

When Christopher Columbus died in 1506, after his fourth voyage across the Atlantic, his body lay for a while in Seville. Because he had declared he did not want to be buried on Spanish soil, his family sent his body to Santo Domingo in what is now the Dominican Republic. When Spain ceded Santo Domingo to France in 1795, remains said to be those of Columbus were sent to Cuba, where they stayed until after the Spanish American War. In 1902, the remains were shipped back across the Atlantic and placed in tomb in Seville's cathedral in front of a massive painting of St. Christopher, the patron saint of travelers. To honor Columbus's wishes, the tomb is raised high above Spanish soil.

In 1877, workers in Santo Domingo found a box containing what they claimed, with significant justification, were the bones of Christopher Columbus. To resolve claims the Seville cathedral had the wrong body, scientists conducted DNA tests on the contents of the Seville tomb. The tests showed a close match with known Columbus descendants, but also revealed that the massive tomb contains less than 200 grams of what one guide describes as a "potpourri" of bone fragments. The Dominicans rejected these tests, but have not tested their bones. Columbus, who departed from Spain and landed near Santo Domingo on his first trip across the Atlantic, may appropriately now rest in both places.

The Sun and the Moon

Portion of Ceiling of Sistine Chapel in Rome, Italy

Visitors to the Sistine Chapel in Vatican City, Italy, often rush through so quickly that they have little time to study Michelangelo's famous frescos on the ceiling. One of those frescos may be evidence of the artist's effort to send a crude message.

By the time he was 29, Michelangelo had already completed the *Pieta*, now in St. Peter's Basilica in Rome, and his extraordinary statue of David, now in Florence's Galeria dell'Accademia, and was already one of most famous artists in Europe. In 1508, Pope Julius II engaged a reluctant Michelangelo to put images on the ceiling of the chapel where new popes are elected. He spent the next four years putting fresco images on the vaulted ceiling that reaches a height of 68 feet. Contrary to popular belief, Michelangelo stood as he painted.

Michelangelo's most famous scene, in the center of the ceiling, shows God almost touching the finger of Adam. In 1990, F. Lynn Meshberger, while a medical student at Indiana University, published an article demonstrating that God's cape and various protruding appendages closely mimic the shape and structures of the human brain. He suggested that Michelangelo, who studied human anatomy, may have intended to show God giving Adam the gift of intelligence.

Most visitors to the Sistine Chapel miss a panel over the altar, showing God creating the sun and the moon. The scene includes what can most delicately be described as a strategically undraped and provocatively directed male *derriere*, apparently that of God. Some speculate that this unusual scene was Michelangelo's way of insulting Pope Julius II for making him spend four years in agony when he wanted instead to be a sculptor. If so, one wonders if the Pope ever got the message. Others piously suggest Michelangelo was illustrating that people are not supposed to see the face of God, a theory that seems a stretch because God's face is shown in the same panel. Or perhaps there is no message—the Sistine Chapel ceiling shows a lot of uncovered flesh reflecting only Michelangelo's virtuosity. Whatever its *raison d'être*, Michelangelo's moon reflects an eternal truth—the greater the artist, the greater the mystery.

Lisbon's Style Setter

Tower of Belém in Lisbon, Portugal

By 1500, Portuguese seafarers had explored the western coast of Africa and sailed around the Cape of Good Hope to India, bringing new ideas and images back to Europe. The iconic Tower of Belém, near where the explorers departed, reflects this unprecedented Age of Discovery.

The Tower of Belém was begun in 1513 when Portugal's King Manuel I ordered a fortress built on a small island in the Tagus River to defend Lisbon's busy port. The king also wanted to salute the Order of Christ, successor to the banned Knights Templar, which had financed many voyages of the Portuguese explorers, including those of members Vasco de Gama and Bartholomew Diaz. The limestone fortress, completed in 1519, comprises a hexagonal bastion facing the river, with openings for cannons on five sides, and an adjoining tower, with a chapel and a room for the king.

The two-part structure, officially named the Tower of St. Vincent after the patron saint of Lisbon, combined images collected by Portuguese explorers from around the world. The silhouette of the four-story tower section evoked temples of eastern India. The twelve melon-domed turrets for small arms and a loggia with seven arches supported on columns drew on Moorish designs. Representations of exotic animals, including what is said to be first rhinoceros seen in Europe, were carved below the turrets. Crosses of the Order of Christ and pyramid-capped designs copied from Moroccan city walls served as merlons. Nautical rope, manifested in stone, bounded the bastion and tower.

The bastion employed more than thick walls for protection. A large statue of the Virgin Mary holding the infant Jesus faced the river from above the cannon openings, seeking to dissuade enemy ships from firing toward the bastion. The strategy failed. In 1580, Spanish forces under the Duke of Abla captured the fortress and used it to house Portuguese prisoners.

The eclectic style of the Tower of Belém became known as Manueline, after King Manuel I, and is considered a transition between Late Gothic and Renaissance architecture. The fortress itself is now a UNESCO World Heritage site and one of the most photographed structures in Portugal.

Sugar Cane and Santeria

City of Trinidad, Cuba

With the increased availability of travel to Cuba, Americans seeking picturesque villages can find them in this hemisphere. Trinidad, Cuba, a UNESCO World Heritage Site famous for its Old World charm, also provides an opportunity to observe the practices of a mysterious New World religion.

Trinidad was founded on December 23, 1514, more than 50 years before St. Augustine, the United States' oldest city. Trinidad became rich trading in both sugar and the slaves needed on nearby plantations. A well-preserved central square, surrounded by red-tiled mansions, reflects that golden age.

With the abolition of slavery, the trade that had supported Trinidad ended and Trinidad clocks seem to have stopped in the nineteenth century. Pastel-colored homes have open windows with only metal bars separating the room inside from the street. Donkeys pull carts down narrow cobblestone streets, pigs roast on wooden spits turned by hand and guitar players sing more for themselves than for tourists.

Slaves from western Africa carried with them the worship of gods (orishas) representing many aspects of their lives. Forced by Spanish masters to practice Roman Catholicism, they cleverly merged their ancestral beliefs with those of Christianity. The resulting syncretic religion is called Santeria (saint worship) because practitioners worshipped the statues of saints, which they had re-identified as their orishas. Many Cubans still call themselves Catholics but practice Santeria at home, some with sacred African images painted on the backs of saints.

Some of the practices of Santeria are closed to outsiders, but others are on display in Trinidad's unique Casa Templo de Santeria Yemaya, a combination museum and house of worship. A blue and white altar pays homage to Yemaya, a goddess of the sea looking a lot like the Virgin Mary. A cigar-smoking Babalawo will, if properly motivated, explain the non-secret aspects of Santeria when not out back conducting services, including sacrifices, for believers.

If you want to see a colorful hillside village where tourists are the primary reminder of the twenty-first century, you have many choices. If you want to experience Santeria, to the extent an outsider ever can, Trinidad may be the best choice.

Protestant Ethic

Town Hall in Zurich, Switzerland

With fewer than 400,000 residents, Zurich, Switzerland, houses the world's second largest gold market and fourth largest stock exchange. Its per capita income is among the highest in the world. Some see Zurich's remarkable economic successes as the legacy of a sixteenth century priest virtually unknown in the United States.

The Romans founded Zurich in 15 B.C. along the Limmat River that flows north from Lake Zurich. The lake and the nearby Glarus Alps whose melting glaciers feed it create one of the most picturesque backdrops of any city in Europe. During the middle ages, Zurich was a self-governing city-state and member of the Swiss Confederacy.

In 1518, Ulrich Zwingli became priest of Zurich's Grossmunster Church. Like Martin Luther, his contemporary in Germany, Zwingli sought to reform the Roman Catholic Church but soon concluded reform was impossible. By 1528 A.D., about half the cities of the Swiss Confederacy had followed Zwingli in rejecting the authority of the Pope. Like the later John Calvin in Geneva, Zwingli preached discipline, thrift and self-reliance, instilling in Zurich what became known as the "Protestant ethic." Many consider Zwingli, killed and mutilated in a major battle between Swiss Catholics and Protestants in 1531, one of the fathers of the Reformation, along with Luther and Calvin.

Under the 1848 constitution creating the Swiss federal government, Zurich became the capital of the Zurich Canton. The city is governed by a citizen assembly meeting in the old town hall curiously located in the river. Influenced by Zwingli, Zurich has long deserved its reputation for efficiency, integrity, prosperity and, some would say, dullness. Zurich has lately cultivated a different side, reportedly now sporting the highest night club density of any city in Europe to go along with its 50 museums.

The marriage of hard work by day with partying by night has succeeded, with recent surveys identifying Zurich as the city having the world's best quality of life. It has also become one of the world's most cosmopolitan cities, with one of every three residents born in another country. The gnomes of Zurich are hiding no more.

The Bones of St. Peter's

St. Peter's Basilica in Rome, Italy

Despite contrary claims, St. Peter's Basilica in Rome remains the world's largest church, featuring the world's tallest dome. Roman Catholics are more inspired by what they believe is its link to the bones of St. Peter, whom they consider their first pope.

In 319 A.D., newly Christian Roman Emperor Constantine ordered a massive basilica built over a small shrine in a cemetery adjacent the Circus of Nero. Local Christians claimed the shrine marked the grave of Peter, the disciple of Jesus they believed was crucified in 64 A.D. The shrine was near an obelisk, plundered from Egypt, at the center of the Circus. Constantine's church, named for Peter, became one of the most important churches in Christendom.

In 1505, the original St. Peter's had fallen into disrepair and Pope Julius II decided to build a new basilica on the site. Numerous designs, all including a dome surpassing Brunelleschi's astounding dome on the Florence Cathedral, were proposed by a series of noted architects, including Rafael. For various reasons, those designs were never built. In 1547, a frustrated Pope Paul III conscripted Michelangelo, then 72, to take over the project and he is credited with creating the overall plan for the current building. In 1586, with construction underway, the obelisk from the Circus of Nero was placed in front of the basilica as a tribute to Peter, with a cross placed atop an apex designed to point toward Egypt's sun god. Completed in 1626, St. Peter's Basilica encloses almost five acres. The signature dome rises 448 feet, 160 feet higher than the United States Capitol dome.

Today, the body of Pope John XXIII is displayed behind glass on the main floor of St. Peter's and that of Pope Saint John Paul II is entombed near Michelangelo's famous *Pieta*. They join at least 89 other popes buried in and under the church that Roman Catholics since Constantine have believed lies over the tomb of St. Peter. In the 1940s, archaeologists uncovered a handful of bones beneath St. Peter's main altar later determined to belong to a man in his 60s. The faithful have no doubt the man's name was Peter.

Cobras on the Square

Snake Charmer in Marrakesh, Morocco

When Marrakesh (or Marrakech) was a stop along the international "hippie trail," Crosby, Stills and Nash sang fondly of "blowing smoke rings" and "charming cobras on the square." Today, smoke rings are harder to find in Morocco's third largest city, but cobras still entertain visitors on the celebrated square.

The Almoravids founded Marrakesh at the foot of the Atlas Mountains in 1062 as the capital of an Islamic empire comprising southern Spain and northwest Africa. The Almohads, practicing a severe form of Islam, conquered Marrakesh in 1147, killing thousands of its citizens and destroying many of its buildings. The Almohads built the Koutubia Mosque over the ruins, its 253-foot-high minaret now a Marrakesh landmark. Marrakesh declined under the Almohads, but entered a period of renewal in the sixteenth century under the Saadi dynasty, which built the magnificent El Badi Palace to mimic the Alhambra in Granada, Spain. The beautiful Saadian tombs, rediscovered in 1917, contain graves of Jewish members of the palace staff mingled with those of the Muslim royal family. In the late nineteenth century, Marrakesh's Grand Vizier built the Bahia Palace for his four wives and 24 concubines in the mudéjar style of Moorish Spain and Morocco.

In the 1960s and 70s, Marrakesh's hashish and hostels attracted members of the counter culture seeking a cheap *kasbah* high. Its aura of authentic oriental mysticism drew the likes of the Rolling Stones, the Beatles and Yves St. Laurent, whose ashes were spread around the restored Marjorelle Garden that he purchased in 1980.

Hashish is now illegal in Marrakesh, a UNESCO World Heritage site. Deluxe hotels and casinos have replaced the flophouses of the hippie era. Visitors come from around the world to see the Koutubia Mosque, the Saadian tombs, the Bahia Palace and Jemaa el-Fnaa, the most famous square in Africa. Reportedly once the site of public beheadings, the square is filled with a noisy collection of exotic entertainers and insistent merchants. For a fee, costumed charmers will make their hooded cobras sway while playing a flute the snakes cannot hear. All aboard the Marrakesh Express!

Center of Understanding

Hall of Private Audiences at Fatehpur Sikri, India

Just a few miles from Agra's famous Taj Mahal, built by the Mughal emperor Shah Jahan, is a much less famous building erected by Akbar, his grandfather. That building and the emperor who designed it are symbols of human tolerance that are now a UNESCO World Heritage site.

Akbar was the grandson of Babur, the founder of the Mughal Empire. He became ruler of a small region in northern India in 1555 at the age of 13 or 14. A few battles later, his empire included much of northern and central India. Although born into a strict Sunni Muslim family, Akbar became fascinated with the different religions of the people living in the lands he had conquered. He was particularly intrigued by a Sufi mystic named Salim Chishti. To honor Salim, Akbar built a magnificent walled city around Salim's camp in the desert west of Agra. Fatehpur Sikri, begun in 1571, became Akbar's capital.

Fatehpur Sikri included a red sandstone building called Diwan-i-Khas or the Hall of Private Audiences where Akbar regularly met with intellectuals representing the many different religions of his empire. Akbar and his guests debated the truth of the claims of their respective religions. From these debates, Akbar concluded that some religious claims were not true. But Akbar also came to believe that all religions reflect common truths. Among these common truths was the value of piety, prudence, abstinence and kindness. Akbar's tolerance of other religions resulted in his abolition of many restrictions that earlier Mughal rulers had imposed on their non-Muslims subjects.

The quest for truth and harmony at Fatehpur Sikri came to a halt after Akbar's death in 1605. Later rulers rejected as heresy his view that all religions contain truths. The entire city was abandoned, probably because its location, far from the nearest river, made supplying adequate water impossible.

The dry desert air helped preserve Fatehpur Sikri and the square building where Akbar demonstrated religious tolerance. Both for that tolerance and his military skill, history has appended "the Great" to Akbar's name. That appellation, rarely used since, awaits a successor.

Domes and Ostrich Eggs

The Blue Mosque in Istanbul, Turkey

The Blue Mosque is one of Istanbul's most popular tourist destinations, often seen as an example of classic Islamic architecture. Like other domed mosques, its design actually mimics a famous church. But its pest control system is undeniably novel.

Ahmed I became Sultan of the Ottoman Empire in 1603, at age 13. After a series of military setbacks, Ahmed sought God's favor by building a mosque in Istanbul to rival the one built in 1558 by Suleiman the Magnificent, his much more successful predecessor. Like Suleiman, Ahmed modeled his mosque on Hagia Sophia, built as a church by Byzantine Emperor Justinian I in 537 A.D. and later converted to a mosque by adding a *mihrab* in the direction of Mecca and minarets. Ahmed's architects lacked the skill (or courage) of those of Justinian, who imaginatively supported the massive dome of Hagia Sophia on its exterior walls. The smaller dome of Ahmed's mosque is supported on four interior columns derided as "elephant legs." Light from more than 200 stained glass windows is supplemented by ornate chandeliers holding uncooked ostrich eggs intended to repel spiders and prevent unsightly webs.

Ahmed surrounded his mosque with six needle-shaped minarets carrying a total of sixteen balconies honoring him as the sixteenth sultan. When Islamic authorities in Mecca learned of the minarets, two more than around both Hagia Sophia and Suleiman's mosque, they were outraged. The Great Mosque in Mecca had six minarets and, as the holiest place in Islam, was not to be out ranked in the minaret department. Ahmed reportedly solved the problem by financing the construction of a seventh minaret in Mecca.

Ahmed died at age 27, a year after completion of his mosque, and was interred in a mausoleum just outside the walls. Although his mosque is officially known as the Sultan Ahmed Mosque, it is popularly known as the Blue Mosque because of 20,000 handmade blue and white tiles in fifty different designs adorning its interior. Still used by Muslim worshippers, the Blue Mosque is open to the public except during daily prayers. Visitors can see for themselves if the ostrich eggs really work.

Magnificent Obsession

The Taj Mahal, near Agra, India

A Nat King Cole love song reciting the splendors of the Taj Mahal is entitled *Magnificent Obsession*. That is an apt description of the story about what many consider the world's most beautiful building and its builder who, for years, could not look at another.

Shah Jahan, ruler of the Mughal Empire of northern India, built the Taj Mahal as a mausoleum for his favorite wife, Mumtaz, who died during the birth of their fourteenth child in 1631. The architectural style blended themes from Persia, Turkey and India. The four minarets at the corners were slanted a few degrees away from the vertical. Whether this was to make sure they do not fall into the building or to create the illusion of being vertical when seen from a distance depends on which guide provides the explanation.

The design of the Taj Mahal and its surrounding gardens evoked the beauty and serenity of Islamic ideas of Paradise. An alternative view of the afterlife is on display nearby, along the sacred Yamuna River on which the Taj Mahal sits. On the banks of this river, Hindus have long cremated their dead, sending their souls back to the gods to be used again.

In 1658, shortly after Shah Jahan had completed the Taj Mahal, he was deposed by his third son, Aurangzeb, who threw his ailing father into the Agra Fort, a picturesque fortress along the Yamuna River. Looking out the single window in his room, Shah Jahan could see only the wide expanse of the river and the Taj Mahal downstream to the right. And so, day after day for eight years, the once powerful emperor stared at his masterpiece, remembered his favorite wife and dreamed of Paradise. When he died in 1666, his body was floated down the river in a simple casket and laid in the Taj Mahal next to Mumtaz, his head turned in the direction of Mecca. Today, more than three million people travel each year to Agra to gaze upon Shah Jahan's magnificent obsession, a UNESCO World Heritage site, and look through the window from which he longed for it.

Beauty and Brains

Company's Garden in Cape Town, South Africa

Cape Town, the second largest city in South Africa, is picturesquely nestled between Table Bay and Table Mountain. Especially on days when a cloud layer known locally as the "table cloth" hovers above its iconic flat-topped mountain, Cape Town is a contender for the most naturally beautiful city in the world. It is also a wonderfully sophisticated city, the equal of any in Europe.

The intellectual center of Cape Town is the Company's Garden, originally used by the Dutch East India Company in the 1650s to grow food for resupplying ships on their way back from India after rounding the Cape of Good Hope. Today, the area is filled with historic statues, immaculately maintained gardens and plenty of over-fed squirrels. Nearby are the Houses of the South African Parliament, the National Library, a planetarium and world-class museums. The Slave Lodge Museum, in a building that once housed slaves adjacent the Company's Garden, recounts a dark side of the garden's history. Some of the Dutch ships picking up supplies dropped off Hindu slaves sold by their Muslim captors to Christian slave traders.

The Iziko South African Museum is located at the south end of the Company's Garden. Founded in 1825, it has become one of the world's finest museums of natural history, housing more than 1.5 million items, including a 70-foot-long skeleton of a blue whale hung from the ceiling. The collection of fossils and skeletons illustrating biological evolution is particularly extensive and insightful. The sign accompanying a very rare skeleton of a lobed-finned fish closely related to the likely progenitor of all four-legged animals acknowledges that "it is difficult to believe that our very distant ancestors were fish similar to the coelacanths." The sign next to the skeleton of Homo sapiens at the end of the evolutionary trail seems especially apt: "The only primate that presents a biological threat to the Earth, and to itself."

Cape Town, with a metropolitan population of almost four million, led the *New York Times* 2014 list of top places to visit. If Cape Town is not on your list of cities to visit, it should be.

Bawdy Days in Luxembourg

Luxembourg Palace in Paris, France

The Luxembourg Palace in Paris, the seat of the French Senate, is the epitome of decorum and elegance. But 300 years ago, the palace was notorious for debauchery and excess by a member of the royal family.

In 1615, Queen Marie de Médicis, the mother and regent of 14-year-old King Louis XIII, built a grand new palace for herself, designed to resemble the Pitti Palace in Florence in which she had been raised. The western wing of the Luxembourg Palace, named for a prior owner of the land, included lavishly decorated rooms for the queen, complete with 24 commissioned paintings by Rubens. The identical eastern wing included rooms for young Louis whenever he visited from his home in the Louvre Palace. When Louis XIII died in 1643, he was succeeded by Louis XIV, who built his own palace at Versailles.

When Louis XIV died in 1715, his famously promiscuous granddaughter, Marie Louise Élisabeth d'Orléans, took up residence in the Luxembourg Palace. Although a recent widow at age 20, she immediately began hosting drunken orgies, glutinous feasts and clandestine lovers. She concealed the resulting pregnancies in her increasing girth, earning the sobriquet "Princess Chubby." When Voltaire suggested that one of the lovers was her father, Philippe II, Duke of Orléans and regent of King Louis XV, he was imprisoned in the Bastille, where he completed his play, *Oedipus*. Oblivious to the irony, Marie Louise, overweight and pregnant, attended the premier with her father, to the great amusement of Parisians. Hard living took its toll and she died, again pregnant at age 23, having already borne five children, none of whom survived.

The orgies behind it, the Luxembourg Palace became a royal museum in 1750, displaying art eventually housed in the Louvre Museum. The palace was confiscated from the royal family during the French Revolution. After serving as the residence of Napoleon, it was enlarged in 1835 to accommodate the semi-circular chambers of the French Senate.

Today, young lovers sit alongside the placid pond south of the palace, watching children sail their little boats. The bawdy days of Princess Chubby are long forgotten.

Virility Record

Moulay Ismail's Stables at Meknes, Morocco

Meknes, a UNESCO World Heritage site, is one of Morocco's former royal cities, along with the better known Fes, Marrakech and Rabat. Meknes is famous for buildings erected by a seventeenth century ruler who fancied himself the equal of French King Louis XIV and holds a world record for virility.

Moulay Ismail ibn Sharif, claiming to be a descendant of Muhammad, became the Sultan of Morocco in 1672. Ismail moved his capital from Fes to Meknes and set about erecting palaces and other buildings to match his image of Versailles. He reportedly used 25,000 slaves in his projects, many of them Europeans captured by Barbary pirates operating from Moroccan ports. Some of the building materials may have been plundered from Volubilis, a nearby city with buildings dating to the time of the Romans.

Ismail's famous stable housed 12,000 horses under a single roof supported by stone arches. Three long corridors intersected at the entrance, allowing one attendant to monitor all the horses simultaneously. An enormous granary adjoining the stable stored grain at controlled temperatures to enable both the horses and the residents to survive a long siege. A wheel inside the granary pulled water from an underground stream. When construction at Meknes was completed, fifteen miles of walls surrounded the city. Ismail, who led huge armies of soldiers from sub-Saharan Africa against his rivals, reportedly placed 10,000 skulls atop the walls to warn prospective attackers.

Ismail maintained good diplomatic relations with Louis XIV, but was rebuffed in his effort to marry Louis' daughter. Not to worry. Ismail had enough wives and concubines to sire at least 867 children. Because of his military successes and his buildings at Meknes, Moulay Ismail is considered one of Morocco's greatest rulers despite (or perhaps because of) his reputation for ruthlessness.

A 1755 earthquake destroyed many of the buildings in Meknes and Ismail's successors moved the Moroccan capital to Marrakech. The stable and granary have been partially restored and they, along with Ismail's mausoleum, are open to visitors. Ismail's record for fathering the most children of any man in history remains untouched.

Street Cows

Street in Jaipur, India

Jaipur, a walled city of about three million people in northwest India, was founded in 1727 by Maharaja Sawai Jai Singh II. It has been known as the "pink city" since 1876, when buildings were painted pink to welcome Prince Edward (later King Edward VII). Jaipur's most famous pink building, the Hawa Mahal (Palace of the Winds), has an intricate sandstone façade representing the crown of Krishna, a Hindu god often given the title of *Gopala*, the Protector of Cows. The cows protected by Krishna wander in and along Jaipur's unusually broad streets, reflecting the Hindu conception of the divine. As Mahatma Gandhi once said, "The central fact of Hinduism is cow protection."

Hindus, constituting about 80 percent of India's population, believe that all sentient beings are animated by an essence called *Atman*, a name related to the English word "atmosphere." They also believe the eternal *Atman* is indistinguishable from Brahman, the transcendent reality underlying all the traditional Hindu gods. As a result, most Hindus are vegetarians and see killing or even corralling animals in the same way they would see doing the same thing to a person or to a god. So, not only do cows roam freely in Indian cities, but so do monkeys and other animals.

Indians revere their cows more than the other animals in their streets because of what cows provide. During its life, a cow provides milk for families, dung for fire and fertilizer and muscles for farms, all without complaint. Upon its natural death, a cow provides skin for shoes and bones for buttons. So important is the cow to the Indian way of life that its name *gau mata* means "mother cow" and ancient Hindu texts refer to the cow as the mother of civilization.

In the crowded streets of Jaipur and other Indian cities, cows block traffic, cause accidents and create chaos in the markets. But efforts to curb their freedom even a little are met with protests. So the cows continue to roam, presenting a living illustration of the Hindu belief that the divine resides in all creatures, great and small.

Hearts and Minds

The Pantheón of Paris

In 1744, King Louis XV promised Madame de Pompadour, his official mistress, a new church honoring St. Genevieve, the patron saint of Paris, if he survived his mysterious illness. He recovered and the resulting Pantheón, named for a pagan temple and honoring the best minds in France, reflects the vagaries of French religious politics.

Louis put his mistress's brother in charge of making good on his promised church. He laid the cornerstone for the building in 1764, the year Madame de Pompadour, famous for her hair style, died. The neoclassical design, in the shape of the Greek cross, drew inspiration from London's St. Paul's Cathedral. Because of a depleted treasury, the church remained unfinished when Louis XV died in 1774. His successor, grandson Louis XVI, loaned his bankrupt government four million francs to finish it.

When the church was finally completed in 1790, it featured a massive triple dome, supported on 258 columns, extending 268 feet above the street. By that time, the French Revolution was in full swing, railing against the power of royalty and the Catholic Church. In 1791, the newly constituted National Constituent Assembly ordered that the church be transformed into a mausoleum honoring French heroes. The building took its new name, meaning "all the gods," from the domed Pantheon in Rome. In 1792, Louis XVI was beheaded for the claimed excesses of his reign.

Twice since 1791, the Pantheón was converted to a church, each time reverting to a mausoleum as sentiments changed. Remains from 50 distinguished French intellectuals, including Voltaire, Rousseau, Victor Hugo and Madame Curie, are now enshrined in the Pantheón's crypt. For six, only their hearts made it, manifesting the practice of removing organs before embalming. The remains of Descartes, whose transfer was authorized in 1792, have yet to arrive.

The United States Capitol architect visited the Pantheón in 1838 and made liberal use of its design concepts in the rebuilt Capitol dome. In 1851, French physicist Leon Foucault demonstrated the Earth's rotation by suspending his famous pendulum from the center of the Pantheón's dome. The democratic rationalists of the French Revolution would be proud.

Morro Castle and
the Fourteenth Colony

Morro Castle in Havana, Cuba

With Americans now able to travel to Havana, they can visit a sixteenth century fortress that played a role in creating an often-overlooked fourteenth English colony.

Spanish explorers founded Havana in 1519 near a natural harbor on the north side of Cuba. Havana soon became the primary port for shipping goods from the New World back to Spain. When gold ships docked in the port proved sitting ducks for Caribbean pirates, Spanish authorities ordered construction of a large fortress on a hill overlooking the narrow entrance to the harbor. The fortress, completed in about 1640, was named *Castillo de los Tres Reyes Magos del Morro* after the Three Magi. Dubbed Morro Castle, the fortress featured an artillery battery called Twelve Apostles pointing toward the water. A chain stretching from Morro Castle to the other side of the harbor entrance blocked pirate ships from penetrating the port.

With its port protected by Morro Castle, Havana grew rich providing supplies for vessels heading for Spain. By the middle of the eighteenth century, Havana was the third largest city in the Americas. In 1762, during its Seven Years' War with France and Spain, England sent 4000 troops to Cuba and captured Morro Castle by attacking it from the unarmed land side, a tactic that apparently caught the Spanish defenders unprepared. Having lost control of the bustling Havana port, Spain ceded Cuba to England. A year later, England traded Cuba back to Spain in exchange for Florida, a deal many in England thought foolish because of the wealth and importance of Cuba. Florida became England's fourteenth American colony, but refused to join the other colonies in seeking independence. In 1783, England returned Florida to Spain in the Treaty of Paris ending the American Revolution.

Today, the well-preserved Morro Castle, part of a UNESCO World Heritage site, is open to the public. Every night at precisely 9:00, guards in Spanish colonial uniforms fire a rusty cannon, a ritual originally intended to signal Havana residents the gates of their city were closing. Few Americans hearing the cannon shots know that the unexpected vulnerability of Morro Castle led to an additional, but short-lived, English colony.

Still Waters

East Side of Mount Vernon, facing the Potomac River

On November 26, 1789, President George Washington issued a proclamation from New York, asking Americans to thank God, for "affording them an opportunity peaceably to establish a form of government for their safety and happiness." Washington himself was most thankful on March 4, 1797, when he ended his second term as President of that government and returned to his beloved Mount Vernon estate.

Washington inherited a half-interest in Mount Vernon, near Alexandria, Virginia, from his half-brother Lawrence, who had named the property after a British admiral. In 1758, before obtaining complete ownership, Washington began enlarging the small farmhouse his father had built overlooking the Potomac River. Upon reaching its current size in 1774, the house encompassed 11,028 square feet and 21 rooms. The exterior was covered by bevel-edged blocks of yellow pine, made to resemble stone by pouring a layer of sand onto wet paint. At Washington's instruction, the weather vane atop a hexagonal cupola featured a dove with an olive branch of peace in its mouth. Washington also designed the two-story piazza facing the river that was widely copied.

At its peak, Washington's Mount Vernon plantation included 8,000 acres, devoted primarily to tobacco and wheat and worked by hundreds of slaves. By 1797 Washington had soured on slavery and upon his death in 1799 he bequeathed the 123 slaves he owned to his wife Martha, with instructions they be freed upon her death. She freed them a year later. Visitors since 1833 have reported a slave cemetery on the property, but surface evidence of it eventually disappeared. On September 21, 1983, the Mount Vernon Ladies Association, owners of the property since 1858, dedicated a cylindrical monument near the tombs of George and Martha Washington to mark the graves of "Afro Americans who served as slaves at Mount Vernon."

Mount Vernon's mansion, outbuildings and 500 remaining acres are open to the public 365 days a year, reflecting Washington's hospitality while living there. Of the more than 80 million visitors since then, only those since 2007 have been able to purchase whiskey from a working replica of Washington's distillery.

Honoring Roman Gods?

West Side of United States Capitol in 2013

The Capitol in Washington, D.C., is among the most-recognizable buildings in the world. Even the name of this symbol of American democracy mirrors European religious buildings, some of them pagan.

In 1791, Pierre L'Enfant, a French-born artist, developed a plan for a new government city along the Potomac River, choosing Jenkins Hill for the "Congress House." Secretary of State Thomas Jefferson renamed both the hill and the proposed building after Rome's Capitoline Hill, the site of the ancient temple to Jupiter Optimus Maximus Capitolinus. Jefferson then suggested that those submitting designs for the new Capitol should evoke the Pantheon, a second century domed temple to all Roman gods. William Thornton, a Scottish-trained physician living in the West Indies, submitted the winning design, incorporating elements of the Pantheon into the section between the legislative chambers, with a low dome centered on columns supporting a classic pediment. These design elements were modified, but all were included in the original Capitol, which was finally completed in 1818 after being damaged in the War of 1812.

By 1850, Congress had outgrown the legislative chambers and approved adding a new chamber at each end of the existing Capitol. The existing dome then appeared too small in relation to the larger building. Thomas Walter based the design of a new dome on the Paris Panthéon, built to honor Genevieve, the patron saint of Paris. Like the Panthéon, the Capitol now incorporates a double dome, the inner section scaled to fit the original rotunda and the outer section scaled to the larger exterior. An oculus atop the inner dome opens to an elaborate fresco inspired by the Panthéon's *Apotheosis of Genevieve*. The *Apotheosis of Washington*, picturing George Washington amidst a number of Roman gods, including Mercury and Venus, was painted by Greek-Italian artist Constantino Brumidi, once employed by Pope Gregory XVI.

Because the cast iron was showing signs of deterioration, the Capitol dome has been under repair since 2014. The history of the dome and illustrations of the Capitol designs since 1792 can be reviewed in the massive underground visitors' center, opened in 2008.

Wool Sacks
and Snuff Boxes

The Palace of Westminster in London, England

The Palace of Westminster, lying along the west bank of the River Thames, is the official name of the building housing England's Parliament. Although most of the eight-acre complex was built in the nineteenth century, its traditions reflect a much longer history.

The original Palace of Westminster, the London home of English kings before becoming the meeting place of Parliament, was almost completely destroyed by fire in 1834. Parliamentary committees rejected proposed classical designs they thought suggested the White House and U. S. Capitol, considered symbols of rebellion. They selected instead a style known as "perpendicular Gothic," with three towers more than 300 feet tall. The building, completed in 1870, includes 1,100 rooms, 100 stairways, three miles of hallways and a shooting range. Big Ben is a bell, housed in the Elizabeth Clock Tower. The Chamber for the House of Commons was rebuilt after being bombed in World War II and intentionally has fewer seats than members.

The building incorporates traditions from earlier eras. The Lord Speaker of the House of Lords sits on a red sack of wool reflecting the central importance of wool to England's medieval economy, a custom dating from the fourteenth century. A box of snuff near the entrance to the Commons Chamber has been kept full since at least the seventeenth century, when smoking was banned. Members of Parliament from opposing parties face each other on historic green-covered benches, with two red lines on the floor between them demarking an area where no one may stand. The lines are said to be two sword lengths apart to prevent dueling. MPs are expected to hang their swords on pink ribbons in the cloak room.

The best time to visit the Palace of Westminster is on Wednesdays, when the Prime Minister fields questions from the Leader of the Opposition, accompanied by heckling and cat calls. The session has gotten less raucous since the questioning time was moved to before lunch, when MPs used to down a pint or two to get ready, but it is still entertaining. Seats in the now shielded Strangers' Gallery are limited, so plan ahead.

In Praise of Iron

Eiffel Tower in Paris, France

In 1887, 300 French writers and artists signed a petition demanding that erection "of this useless and monstrous Eiffel Tower" be halted immediately. What the petitioners called "a giddy, ridiculous tower dominating Paris like a gigantic black smokestack" has become a beloved symbol of Paris, each year attracting almost seven million visitors, more than any other paid monument in the world.

The Eiffel Tower is named for Gustave Eiffel, a French engineer who gained fame in 1880 for his innovative design for an iron truss skeleton for the Statue of Liberty, replacing the planned masonry core. Maurice Koechlin, a member of Eiffel's firm who worked on that design, learned of a need for an entrance arch near the left bank of the Seine for a world's fair commemorating the 100th anniversary of the French Revolution. He and colleague Émile Nouguiera proposed an iron lattice arch extending into a tower 300 meters high, far taller than any man-made structure. Initially lukewarm, Eiffel eventually championed the idea of showing the capabilities of iron for very tall structures. His firm's design, enhanced by Nouguiera, was selected in 1886. When the Eiffel Tower was completed in 1889, it nearly doubled the height of the Washington Monument, built entirely of stone.

As originally approved, the Eiffel Tower was to be disassembled after 20 years and its 7300 tons of iron and 2.5 million rivets sold as scrap. But Gustave Eiffel had other ideas. Soon after the tower's opening, he began inviting scientists to use it for experiments requiring great heights. In 1919, as the permit was to expire, antennae atop the tower began sending radio signals throughout France and the Eiffel Tower earned a permanent place in the Parisian skyline.

The Eiffel Tower remained the world's tallest man-made structure until the Chrysler Building surpassed it in 1930, incorporating a steel skeleton pioneered by William Le Baron Jenney, an engineering classmate of Gustave Eiffel in Paris. Today, thanks to Eiffel and his classmate, no one would think of building a tall structure without the "hateful column of bolted sheet metal" disparaged by Eiffel's nineteenth century critics.

World War Class

Shrine Room in Indiana War Memorial in Indianapolis

As we travel to see the world's treasures, we can overlook those in our own back yards. The Indiana War Memorial is just such a treasure, often ignored by people driving by it every day.

In 1920, as part of a successful plan to lure the American Legion headquarters to Indianapolis, the Indiana General Assembly appropriated $2 million for a monument to the victors of the recent world war. General John J. Pershing broke ground for the 210-foot-tall War Memorial in 1927, which was dedicated in 1933 even though the interior remained incomplete despite additional funding from the Works Progress Administration.

The design of the three-story square building, with columns and pyramid-shaped roof, evokes the tomb of Mausolus, a wonder of the ancient world that gave us the word "mausoleum." Words carved in the limestone exterior express hope the building will "inspire patriotism and respect for the laws to the end that peace may prevail, justice be administered, public order maintained and liberty perpetuated."

The building's surprisingly capacious interior, making extensive use of marble, includes a 500-seat auditorium, meeting rooms and a museum of military history. The inspiring Shrine Room on the third floor honors the soldiers who won the "war to end all wars." Incorporating materials from all the Allies, the room features a huge American flag hanging vertically over an Altar of Consecration. The altar is surrounded by 24 fluted columns of dark red Vermont marble. High above the altar are blue lights and a crystal Star of Destiny from Sweden. Wall paintings depict the leading Allied soldiers. Marble stairways to the Shrine Room contain the names of all Hoosiers who served in World War I.

The Indiana War Memorial garnered national attention in 1953 when Edward R. Murrow's popular *See it Now* television series covered the American Legion's controversial closing of the auditorium to the Indiana Civil Liberties Union. Those days are long gone and the building is open to the public Wednesdays to Sundays from 9 am to 5 pm. The next time you long to visit a world-class building, consider a trip to the Indiana War Memorial.

History in a Havana Hotel

Hotel Nacional in Havana, Cuba

The 10-story building overlooking the Havana Harbor bears an intentional resemblance to a famous Florida hotel. The Cuban version has had a much more colorful past than its American relative.

Havana's Hotel Nacional (National Hotel) lies on the site of an old battery near the seawall separating Havana from the Caribbean. Reportedly financed by mobsters using bootlegging earnings, the luxury hotel was planned in the 1920s to accommodate the growing number of Americans traveling to Havana to drink, gamble and ogle showgirls. The New York firm of McKim, Mead and White designed the hotel to mimic the Breakers in Palm Beach, Florida, its own design aping Rome's Villa Medici. About 8000 workers built the 426-room hotel, which opened in 1930 and became the favorite of gangsters, movie stars and assorted notables, including Lucky Luciano, Meyer Lansky, Errol Flynn, Rita Hayworth, Jean-Paul Sartre and Ernest Hemingway.

In 1933, during the Revolt of the Sergeants, junior army officers led by a young Fulgencio Batista launched a bloody attack against senior officers living luxuriously in the hotel. In December 1946, 500 representatives of organized crime families met at the hotel for a six-day summit organized by Luciano and hotel owner Lansky, who shared the hotel's gambling profits with Batista. Frank Sinatra provided the entertainment for the infamous conclave, fictionalized in *Godfather Part II*. After overthrowing American-supported Batista in 1959, Fidel Castro nationalized the hotel and closed its famous casino and bawdy cabaret. Castro and Che Guevara used the hotel as their headquarters during the Cuban Missile Crisis, protected by anti-aircraft guns positioned on the grounds. Castro refurbished the hotel in the 1990s to help expand Cuban tourism and an anti-Castro group seeking to damage the economy bombed the hotel in 1997.

Today, the land on which the Hotel Nacional sits, complete with shore cannons, is a UNESCO World Heritage site. The hotel's Churchill Bar reflects Winston Churchill's 1946 stay and a bust of Nat King Cole remembers his 1957 performances after earlier being refused entrance to the hotel because of his race. Mirroring eight decades of Cuban history, the hotel remains a sentimental favorite of Russian diplomats.

Keep Calm and Carry On

24 HOURS G 0600 S FROM 6 TO 0 INCL.	PLOTTED	CROSSED COAST	OVER LONDON	DESTROYED				CASUA	
				FTRS	A.A.	BLNS	TOTAL	FATAL	SE
	3966	2966	1473	1148	387	107	1642	3802	10
21	90	72	40	21	11	4	36		
22	207	144	69	10	29	13	52		
23	156	96	43	48	24	8	80		
24	93	66	22	35	13	2	50		
25	62	47	26	12	4	3	19		
26	46	38	16	15	13	3	31	415	14
27	105	75	25	54	25	4	83		
28	151	115	57	40	23	3	66		
29	119	84	40	32	35	3	70		
30	134	99	42	22	41	1	64		
31	95	62	29	20	8	2	30		
1	34	26	17	7	5	2	14		
2	81	53	32	1	17	4	22	508	14
3	219	154	92	7	33	18	58		
4	193	119	40	57	58	9	124		
5	149	102	35	44	53	7	104		
6	126	73	23	41	30	8	70		

V-1 Casualty Reports from Churchill War Rooms in Westminster, England

Every December 7, Americans remember the 1941 attack on Pearl Harbor that brought war to the United States. By then, England had been suffering major attacks for more than a year. The courage of English citizens during the horrors of World War II is on display in the Churchill War Rooms in Westminster, now open to the public.

In August 1939, days before the German invasion of Poland, the English government opened a command center beneath a new public office building now housing the Treasury. The underground complex included a Cabinet room, a map room, bedrooms for staff, rooms for clerks and a room for secure communications with international leaders. In October 1940, after the onset of German bombing of London, a five-foot-thick ceiling was added to make the facility secure against aerial attack and the Cabinet began meeting underground. The complex also included a bedroom, outfitted with communications gear, for Prime Minister Winston Churchill. Although Churchill gave four wartime speeches from the bedroom, he rarely slept there, preferring to spend his evenings with his wife Clementine at 10 Downing Street.

After the surrender of Japan in 1945, the command center was abandoned. It was opened to the public in 1984, the rooms presented as they were at war's end. Papers still lie on the Cabinet room tables and colored pins pierce a large map, showing the front lines of opposing armies. One wall chart includes an obscene hand-drawn picture of Adolph Hitler. Another chart shows the effect of the V-1 attacks that began after the Allied invasion of Normandy. With numbers carefully written by hand, the chart records almost 3000 "flying bombs" crossing the English coastline between June 16 and July 20, 1944, killing 3802 civilians and seriously injuring another 10,936, more than American losses at Pearl Harbor.

A museum was added to the War Rooms in 2005, displaying a bust of Churchill, looking very much the bulldog. The gift shop sells items bearing the iconic wartime slogan "Keep Calm and Carry On." The Churchill War Rooms provide lessons in English resolve that can find application anytime and anywhere.

Home of Independence

Sabarmati Ashram at Ahmedabad, India

Ahmedabad is the world's third fastest growing city. Despite needing residential land, the Indian government has reserved prime real estate along Ahmedabad's central river as a memorial to the man Indians revere as the Father of the Nation.

In 1915, after working 21 years in South Africa as a lawyer, Mohandas Gandhi came to Ahmedabad to employ his ideas of non-violent resistance in support of Indian independence. In 1917, he acquired 36 acres of wasteland along the west bank of the Sabarmati River and built an "ashram" on the previously snake-infested site. He and his followers lived together at the ashram seeking truth while practicing Gandhi's ideals of discipline, chastity, religious tolerance, self-reliance and non-violence. One of Gandhi's objectives was demonstrating that Indian people did not need to rely on the British, so he and his followers made their own cloth and grew their own food. In 1930, while living at the ashram, Gandhi organized a 241-mile march to the sea protesting the British salt tax. The event eventually led to the arrest of 60,000 people and galvanized the Indian public in support of independence. After the march, the British government seized Gandhi's ashram.

India received its independence in August 1947. Five months later, before Gandhi could return to the ashram, he was assassinated by a Hindu nationalist who thought his teachings were too tolerant of Muslims. The government now maintains the tranquil, tree-filled grounds of the Sabarmati Ashram as a shrine to the person Indians now call Mahatma, the Great Soul. Some of Gandhi's simple personal possessions are exhibited in the small house where he lived for 12 years with his wife Kasturba. A museum houses his letters, writings and pictures and displays some of his most famous teachings, including, "If blood be shed, let it be our own" and "Forsake not truth, even unto death." The museum also displays the folding spinning wheel that Gandhi encouraged Indians to use to reduce their dependence on British imports.

The Sabarmati Ashram is Ahmedabad's most popular destination. For admirers of Gandhi's philosophy of tolerance and non-violence, it should be part of any trip to India.

Hardship and Inspiration

Quarry on Robben Island, South Africa

Guided tours of notorious prisons can be entertaining, as known by anyone who has listened to the Beefeaters at the Tower of London. But a tour of the prison on Robben Island is a far different experience, providing insights about the man who spent 18 years there on his way to becoming the president of South Africa.

Robben Island is located in Table Bay about five miles from Cape Town. Since the earliest days of the Dutch settlers, Robben Island has been used as a warehouse for people not wanted on the mainland. A guided bus trip around the island points out cell blocks and a cemetery for lepers that give silent testimony to the plights of people who lived and died there.

Today Robben Island is known worldwide because of a single prisoner. In 1964, Nelson Mandela was sent to Robben Island for his role in encouraging acts of sabotage against the white-only government. While there, he was consigned to the infamous limestone quarry a 20-minute walk from the prison. He was forced to work day after day against a bright rock face removing stone for use in island roads, with the glare and dust permanently damaging his eyes. But Mandela did more than swing a limestone pick. He took control of the younger activists who were also there for participating in acts against the government. So influential was Mandela in teaching and inspiring these prisoners that Robben Island became known as "Mandela University." Perhaps to deprive the students of their teacher, Mandela was transferred to another prison in 1982, from which he was finally released in 1990 in an event televised around the world.

Former inmates now act as guides at Robben Island, showing visitors Mandela's eight by seven foot cell furnished with a bucket, a small table, straw sleeping mats and some blankets. They also tell stories about the lessons of discipline and patience they learned from the man who eventually became the leader of their country.

Cape Town is a beautiful city, but the tour to Robben Island, a UNESCO World Heritage site, makes the trip really memorable.

Symbol of Unity

Berlin's Brandenburg Gate from the West

Brandenburg Gate was a symbol of division. It is now a symbol of German pride and unity.

In about 1788, Prussian King Frederick William II ordered construction of a monument to peace at the western end of the Unter den Linden, a tree-lined boulevard that led to his palace. His architects designed an 85-foot-high triumphal arch modeled on the entrance to the Athens Acropolis. The 213-foot-wide gate, now known as the Brandenburg Gate, was completed in 1791. Six pairs of Doric columns form five passageways, the center one originally reserved for royalty. The chariot of the quadriga atop the arch was formerly driven by Eirene, the Greek goddess of peace. When the Prussians defeated Napoleon in 1814, they replaced Eirene with Victoria, the winged goddess of victory.

The Brandenburg Gate lies along Ebertstraße, a north/south street that formed part of the boundary between the Western and Russian sectors when the Allies partitioned Berlin after World War II. When East Germany erected the Berlin Wall in 1961, the wall extended along Ebertstraße, placing the Brandenburg Gate just inside East Berlin. Travel of any kind through the gate was banned and the Brandenburg Gate became an immediate symbol of resistance to a divided Berlin.

On June 26, 1963, President John Kennedy spoke just west of the gate, uttering the now famous words, "*Ich bin ein Berliner*" ("I am a Berliner"). On June 12, 1987, President Ronald Reagan, with his back to the Brandenburg Gate, demanded that Soviet Leader Mikhail Gorbachev "open this gate" and "tear down this wall." Twenty-nine months later, the wall fell. On December 22, 1989, the Brandenburg Gate reopened.

Today, the Brandenburg Gate is accessible only to pedestrian traffic and opens onto Pariser Platz, a public square where Berliners celebrate their freedom and unity. Residents traveling past the Brandenburg Gate are reminded of their past by more than a dozen white crosses hanging on a fence aside the Ebertstraße. Each cross bears the name of a person killed trying to cross the street that once divided the now-united city.

Index

About the Author

Donald E. (Don) Knebel earned a degree in electrical engineering from Purdue University and a law degree from Harvard University. Having retired from the active practice of law at the end of 2013 after 39 years as an intellectual property litigator, he now serves as Adjunct Professor and Senior Advisor at the Center for Intellectual Property Research at the Indiana University Maurer School of Law. He has been very active in the Indianapolis community, where he served as chair of the 2010 United Way Campaign. Don and his wife Jen, a certified lay pastor, have traveled extensively in Europe, the Middle East, India and elsewhere, seeking a better understanding of the world's religions and cultures. Don is a frequent speaker on religious history, comparative religion, politics of the Middle East and the First Amendment. In 2015, he was named "Interfaith Ambassador of the Year" by the Center for Interfaith Cooperation, an organization he helped found in 2012 to develop a better understanding among people of different religious beliefs. The stories in this book are selected and edited from a weekly column he has written for the *Current* newspapers since early 2012.